ODYSSEYS

Selected Short Stories & Poems

———————

By Donna De Leo Bruno

Odysseys
Selected Short Stories & Poems

By
Donna DeLeo Bruno

Visit our website at www.StillwaterPress.com for more information.
First Stillwater River Publications Edition
ISBN-10: 1-946-30004-7
ISBN-13: 978-1-946300-04-1

1 2 3 4 5 6 7 8 9 10
Written by Donna DeLeo Bruno
Published by Stillwater River Publications, Glocester, RI, USA.

Dedication

T here were many who nurtured my intense love of reading and writing, as well as my keen appreciation of literature. First and foremost was my mother, Martha DiMezza DeLeo, whose first gift when I was born was a complete set of red leather bound classic stories for children from which she faithfully read to me and my sister each and every day when we were growing up. Then there were the Filippini nuns at Our Lady of Mt. Carmel School, where each Friday I would eagerly anticipate the arrival of *The Little Messenger*, the most delightful children's newspaper which was our treat following a week's completion of demanding lessons. It was at this elementary parochial school that I first responded emotionally to literature. In 7th grade, I recall reading Longfellow's epic poem *Evangeline* which focuses on the invasion of a close-knit community in Arcadia (Nova Scotia) just before the wedding of two lovers. The setting of this idyllic pastoral is poetically described in beautifully rhythmic, lilting verse; and the story of the couple who are separated and exiled just as they are to begin their life together is heart-breaking. I remember being so emotionally affected as the couple spend a life-time searching for each other, the suspense prolonged as each misses the other by mere days. At the end

i

Evangeline, who has devoted her life to serving God as a nun, finds her beloved Gabriel on his deathbed, too late. I was so moved by the sad story, as well as the poet's skillful use of dactylic rhythm -- its musical, mellifluous quality -- that I have never forgotten its impact on me. I did not know about the artistic use of various poetic rhythms at that young age; I just knew that it was melodious to my ears and stirring to my heart. These years were followed by high school at Bristol, Rhode Island's Colt Memorial where, in my junior year, Dr. Paul Fletcher decided to stage a performance of Shakespeare's *A Midsummer Night's Dream*, a very novel approach at that time. I was selected for the role of the fairy Puck. And so began my acquaintance with "The Bard," whose genius I came to appreciate more fully under the tutelage of Professor Frank Greene at Rhode Island College. While studying Shakespearean plays with him in class, he would actually close his eyes, so impressed by an exquisite line, kiss his fingertips, raise them to the air in tribute and exclaim, "Beautiful! Simply beautiful!" Also at Rhode Island College was Dr. Devine with whom I studied "Authors of the Victorian Age." An incurable romantic, I was in heaven -- the poetry of Elizabeth Barrett and Robert Browning, *Wuthering Heights* by Emily Bronte, the novels of Charles Dickens, particularly *Great Expectations,* all of which I loved and taught myself to hundreds of students in my Literature and Writing courses at Barrington High School (Rhode Island). Later at the University of Rhode Island, I began postgraduate work which continued at Providence College, where I had the good fortune to study Geoffrey Chaucer's *The Canterbury Tales* in Olde English (a foreign language) under the guidance of a professor on leave from Brown University and loaned for the summer for his expertise on that particular work. Even a course that same summer at Providence College on John Donne's metaphysical poetry -- very heavy stuff! -- did not dampen my enthusiasm. Later at Roger Williams University, my awareness of gender modeling was heightened with analysis of the reading texts provided for elementary students, primarily the *Dick and Jane* series on which I myself had been weaned. Although even in those earliest first, second, and third grades, I had loved reading about Jane cooking in the kitchen with mother, baking cookies and the like, while Dick was actively engaged in outer oriented activities -- riding his bike, scouting around exploring -- I had not been aware of the subliminal messages in these "benign" learning tools. How could I be? I was a child devouring all reading matter to which I was exposed --

unaware that I was simultaneously learning social mores -- what be-havior was appropriate for girls and which was suitable for boys.

And so this multitude of learning experiences have contributed to the bibliophile and writer I am today -- thoroughly engaged in the action of a book; aware of the various techniques employed by authors to seamlessly weave together intriguing plots; to portray complex and unforgettable characters who fascinate and evoke our emotions; to use symbolism in developing themes; to stimulate deep and serious think-ing; to enrich, educate, inform and inspire. My most sincere gratitude to all of them for "I am indeed a part of all that I have met." (from poem *Ulysses* by Alfred Lord Tennyson)

Introduction

Although the stories in this collection seem unrelated -- set in very different locales -- there **IS** a common theme -- "odysseys." All involve a sort of wandering or trip which results in a personal transformation for each of the individual characters.

In the first entitled *Adventure in Corsica*, a woman experiencing conflict in her marriage, finds romantic respite on that rocky Mediterranean island.

In the second, *Westward, Ho!* a young female pioneer, following an extremely traumatic attack, finds renewal in the person of a Lakota Indian hero.

Next, in *Donatella Annunziata Concetta D'Alessandro*, an insecure Italian girl must travel from Federal Hill, an ethnic conclave in Providence, Rhode Island, to a small village on Italy's Amalfi Coast to find her "real" home and a sense of identity.

In *Copy-Cat*, a pampered woman finds her way back to an old friendship destroyed long ago by pettiness.

The word *odyssey* is defined as a journey filled with notable experiences for the individual, and in a sense, that is true for each of my characters in the stories featured in this book.

ADVENTURE IN CORSICA

ADVENTURE IN CORSICA
A Mediterranean Interlude

They'd agreed at last on one thing -- a change of scene might have an improved effect upon their testy moods. About to book flights, they still negotiated back and forth in the relentless tug-and-pull that was their marriage. He favored the sandy, lazy beaches of the Caribbean, while she preferred a more exotic location -- specifically the rugged, rocky coast of a Mediterranean island. Her stubborn victory placed them on wind-swept Corsica, impressive in its stark and barren wildness. While he opted for a guided scuba dive exploring a plane submerged since WWII, she ventured to explore a remote village at the peak of the mountain. After traversing by jeep an extremely precipitous and deeply-rutted incline, Amelia found herself at the peak, in what appeared to be a medieval square circled by ancient constructions built centuries ago.

Suspended from a rickety scaffold above, a laborer was attempting to repair a church tower, laboriously hoisting stone by stone in a pulley apparatus, then securing each in place with mortar. Even the time-worn bucket of cement was precariously raised and lowered for refill by a fraying rope. A wrinkled gnome-like creature, swathed entirely in black, crouched bent upon the rim of the town's circular well where locals came with gaily painted terracotta pitchers to obtain their daily supply of water. Once all had filled their jugs to over-flowing, Amelia focused her camera upon the wizened figure by the well, hoping to capture a provincial shot of local color. Grabbing her gnarled cane, the old hag lunged threateningly toward the photographer, screaming shrilly a sort of chant in an unknown tongue, lashing at her with the stick. In her fall backwards, Amelia was relieved to be caught by supportive, muscular arms that steadied her.

"Signora," he cautioned, "you must be careful. You do not know the customs here. The old woman is superstitious, believing the camera would draw her soul from out her body. Capisce? You understand?" He spoke English, but with an unusual accent, rolling the r's so that the word underline camera came out "kar-merr-ah."

"You are Italian?" she asked.

"Italian and Greek," he replied. "You are a bit shaky. Would you care to take a seat and have a drink here at the cafe?" He introduced himself as Eduardo.

Choosing a circular iron table inlaid with brilliant mosaics, Amelia saw the glazed cobalt tiles contrasted against the eye-catching sunflower yellows, creating a dazzling, vibrant kaleidoscopic design. After their drinks were served, his bronzed hand lifted his glass in a toast to "Daring adventures!"

After some small talk, he offered to give her a tour of the locale. Realizing that he was a total stranger and she in a strange land where caution should prevail, Amelia politely demurred, thanking him for saving her from a fall earlier, as well as for the refreshing beverage.

The day lay ahead of her; and always a curious traveler, she progressed on nimble legs in her ascent upward and upward still, through cobbled, winding alleys, a labyrinth of twists and turns. She had read in guidebooks that the "adventure" was to become lost in the maze of such places in order to fortuitously come upon some hidden gems. Though isolated, the town was naturally lush -- violet bougainvillea cascaded over high ancient stone walls, the azure sea stretched far below, providing a sparkling panorama of brilliant blue as far as the eye could see. She wondered at what spot her husband might be swimming beneath this water, but she was glad to be alone to savor this wandering on her own.

Farther in her roaming, she came upon a crumbling chapel, overgrown with moss and twisted vines, but charming in its simplicity. Gingerly placing her sandaled feet on each uneven stepping stone to its entrance, she gave the battered door a push and entered. Always the romantic, she chose a dusty, splintered pew and rested, imagining the nuptials and ardent vows exchanged at the front altar. Allowing her imagination free rein, she wondered if these couples had fared better than she in their choice of a spouse, even though she had wed freely; while many of the pairings of these earlier couples were likely arranged by parents and guardians, as was the custom in times past. Crossing herself, she said a prayer since in parochial grammar school the nuns had promised that a wish requested in an unknown church would be granted. Enough of contemplating such things, she rose to exit. Once outside, just as she was to begin the long descent, she sensed a long peripheral shadow fall across her path before being swallowed up in utter darkness. Wrapped in a smothering blanket, she was dragged backwards, struggling against her captor. Suddenly she caught a whiff of a noxious odor and all her limbs went numb.

Regaining consciousness in a dim and barren cave, she found herself fettered to an iron ring embedded in the rocky wall. The length of chain secured to it allowed her movement, but to where? In dazed shock, she realized she was a prisoner, taken unawares. And then she saw him -- tall, lanky, muscular, bronzed -- her acquaintance of earlier in the piazza. Smiling sardonically, he offered her a metal cup of cool water which she gulped greedily. Her throat was parched and all her bones ached.

From the shadows a smaller, rugged man emerged, ogling her lasciviously with a critical sneer.

"Why am I here?" she demanded. And when neither replied, she repeated in Italian, "Perché sono qui?"

Rather than responding to her question, the handsome Eduardo stepped forward.

"Hai fame?" he solicitously asked, extending a basket of grapes, figs, and oranges.

Indeed, she was ravenously hungry, despite the remnants of grogginess and disorientation.

They fed her well -- Arturo, the short and stocky one, had procured the best olives from the Peloponnese and deliciously sharp cheeses from the Italian Parma region. She was a bit of a culinary expert herself. In addition, there was incredibly fresh "pesce" which Eduardo boasted he had caught himself, spearing them from his "barca." The tantalizing aroma from the iron grate outside wafted into the cave entrance.

"You are too skinny, Signora," observed the Italian/Greek Adonis, as he extended the tin plate to her from his outstretched hand. "We prefer some flesh upon our women. Mangia!"

He alternated between English and Italian as it suited him. It seemed perverse in such a situation, but she found his accent appealing, particularly the tongue-rolling of his r's, speaking in the most mellifluous Italian -- a language she adored. Even his lips curled sensuously as he formed the letters.

"I must be insane," she reprimanded herself silently, "or suffering a concussion." Amelia knew that she should be quaking in terror, but somehow she felt no danger, rather an other-worldly sense of pleasant displacement. Eduardo's charming demeanor and gentlemanly courtesy had overcome any trepidation that would have been more normal under the circumstances. It was the peasant-faced Arturo with his impatient manner who unsettled her. Spewing guttural orders, he rarely looked directly at her; and she could sense his bitterness when Eduardo passed to her the meatiest portion of fish. Resentment and annoyance were deeply etched on his unshaven, weather-beaten visage, and he made some crude remark of disgust.

Although not fluent in the language, she was later able to decipher through their whispered conversation that money was involved -- perhaps a ransom -- she could not be sure. After she had been there a few days, she observed volatile Arturo trudge out at sunrise, returning at dusk from far below with provisions, a "gior-nale," and - once or twice -- a letter. The contents of the newspapers or the letters occasionally caused disagreement or argument, as Ar-turo gesticulated violently, raising his voice and fists threateningly to Eduardo; and on one occasion stormed outside, kicking over the spit of lamb roasting over the fire. Eduardo appeared nonplussed, rescuing the soot-covered meat and preparing a salad, surrounded artistically with red roasted peppers which Arturo had brought back yesterday. They ate together -- just the two of them -- beneath the starlit sky -- and later, from the back of the cave, he retrieved a well-used, bruised mandolin on which he played, with slender, graceful fingers, the sweetest ethnic melodies. Lulled into a peaceful slum-ber, she never saw Roberto return that night.

Unaware exactly how many days had passed, she estimated it had been about a month since her "abduction." It seemed odd to mentally summon that word, since as time elapsed, she found she had never felt so rested. At home she was a fitful sleeper, tossing and turning, awakening numerous times a night. Yet here the salu-brious mountain air and quiet, natural landscape of this Eden-like setting seemed to soothe her. Moreover, she eagerly anticipated dusk when a navy-blue sky provided a vast background for the glit-tering celestial shapes that so intrigued Eduardo. In Arturo's frequent absence, Eduardo would lead her outside; and summoning his best English, attempted to tutor her about the galaxy, delineating with his index finger first Orion, then Ursa Minor, Ursa Major -- tracing their ethereal starlit shapes. Again his exaggerated pronunciation of the last "m-a-h-r-j-o-o-r" provoked laughter. When the air chilled, he ceremoniously wrapped a coarse-haired woolen blanket round her shoulders, added embers to the campfire while she feasted her eyes upon his masculine shape, starkly silhouetted in the moonlight. Ra-ther than the nightmares of a prisoner ignorant of her future, her dreams consisted of unrequited yearnings.

Something altered around this time. In the second month of captivity, Arturo was absent for longer periods of time. Eduardo had been ushering her on long explorations -- "for exercise," he sug-gested. But on this particular morning, he approached her with a more gleeful expression. With inviting arms outstretched, he helped her to rise. Grinning broadly, he offered, "Oggi facciamo la passeggiata." Willingly, she took his hand and held it steadfastly as he guided her from out the depth of the charcoal dark cave. In the bright daylight, the dazzling sun created glittering diamond-like prisms on the shimmering sea below. As they jumped from boulder to boulder, she observed his black and lustrous "Sampson" curls bounce playfully around his ears and long tanned neck; and when he turned backward to teasingly urge her forward, the ebony locks fell like silken spiral ribbons across his tanned forehead. She found herself returning his smile, and her heart felt light. Ignoring her repeated inquiries, "Dove` andiamo?" (Where are we going?) he replied "Pazienza, Carina. Pazienza." (Patience, my dear one, patience). This was the endearment used many years ago by her grandparents. "Dear one" pronounced in his sensual voice sounded heavenly to her ears and stirred something -- long dormant -- deep within her. Skipping gingerly among the rocks, a flat outcropping appeared between the boulders -- a sort-of private mesa. Releasing his warm grasp, he dropped the wicker basket, removed a large cobalt blue and dandelion yellow tablecloth, which he shook open and spread upon the rock slab. Its whimsical paisley pattern delighted her, and she searched for smaller rocks to secure the corners. Upon this he spread his bounty -- a generous hunk of extra sharp provolone cheese, spicy soppressata, a log of dried pepperoni, and a crusty loaf of Sicilian bread.

Appearing to be enjoying himself immensely, he took pains to unwrap the vittles slowly and arrange them in an artful display. As he prolonged the drama, she studied his movements, his gestures -- the raised, arched muscled arms extended to the sky as if to say, "Look and behold our feast!"

Everything about him exuded masculine physicality. Now spread out comfortably on the wide cloth, he leaned back to take a bottle of red wine from the basket to uncork it.

"What do you call deese in Ah-merr-e- kah? Pick -e-neek?"

She couldn't help but giggle in return to the playful ear-to-ear smile he bestowed upon her.

"Something like that," she agreed, but corrected his pronunciation - "p-i-c-n-i-c."

He poured the claret-colored liquid in two glasses, swirling them as would a sommelier in an upscale restaurant. Given this wild setting, this too amused her, and it seemed so very long ago she'd laughed so heartily and spontaneously. He actually fed her a morsel of cheese which she nibbled slowly, allowing its strong flavor to sting her taste-buds. Her whole body felt on high alert, her senses eager for stimulation. Draping a sweet pepper on her finger, she placed it upon his extended tongue, the warm saliva coating her hand. She could detect a rhythmic pulsation in his neck in synchrony with the metronomic beating of her heart. The wine enhanced the tastes upon her palate, sliding smoothly, warmly, languorously down her throat. Again and again, he filled their glasses until she felt the warmth in her belly and a heady dizziness. She yearned to freeze forever this intensely unique and highly-charged moment. And then these weeks of smoldering tension peaked as she impulsively leaned forward to kiss him fully, unreservedly, luxuriating in those irresistible lips. His arms surrounded her in a trembling, passionate embrace. With her chin rested upon his shoulder, she spied in the distance Arturo shouldering a rifle, plodding laboriously up the steep slope, his face a vermillion contortion of rage and fury, evident even from this distance. Startled to her senses, she gasped; and Eduardo turned to see what had caused her to rigidly withdraw from him.

Placing his finger to his lips to silence her, he rapidly gathered up the cloth, glasses, bottles and stashed them out of sight. Instructing her to follow him, they began their descent and arrived at their "abode" just moments ahead of Arturo. What ensued not only summoned Amelia's apprehension but effected a return to reality. A visibly shaken Arturo hurled a "giornale" (newspaper) at Eduardo, bellowing stridently a volcanic tirade from which she could comprehend only a few words; "carbinieri e polizia" (police), "soldi" (money), "un milione" (one million), "Siamo tutto finiti" (We are finished - it is over). "Basta!" (enough). "Questo era uno sbaglio" (This was a mistake) -- "il pegggio" (the worst). "Ho paura" (I am frightened). E` necessario ... (It is necessary ...) and then somewhere in all this wild rambling --"morte" (death). His, theirs, hers -- she did not know?

She had begun to tremble as she observed Eduardo's ineffectual attempts to calm him.

"Aspetta!" (Wait). Dobbiamo rimanere calmi." (We must remain calm). "Decidero` io quello che faremo." (I will decide what to do).

But Arturo would not be placated. Wringing his twisted hands, he screamed, "E` necessario distuggere tutto qui." (It is necessary to destroy everything here). "Sbrigati!" (Hurry)! "Non e` possibile riparare questo." (There is no fixing this).

He was hysterical now, his hands shaking, his eyes glazed. "Ci penso io della donna." (I will deal with the woman). "Subito! Subito!" (Immediately/Now), and then he reached violently for Amelia, brutally dragging her toward the opening.

Unexpectedly, she felt his viselike grasp of her arm released, as Arturo collapsed in a thudding heap. There was no time to discern what felled him, but Eduardo indiscriminately grabbed blankets, a goat-skin of water, and various edibles which he tossed in a woven bag. Pulling her roughly behind him, he began the long descent. She stumbled over rocks and staggered breathless, stung by briars and nettles in their path; but Eduardo did not stop. He seemed impervious to pain, tenacious in his grasp on her hand; but when it seemed she could not go on, gasping for breath, bruised and bleeding, he lifted her over his shoulder and proceeded downward like a man possessed. As dusk fell, he found a small outcropping of succulent bushes, and gently lowered her there upon the blanket he had spread. Against his shoulder, he lifted her head and from the goatskin drizzled liquid between her lips, caressing them softly with his calloused thumb. She seemed to rally; and holding her to a sitting position, he fed her tiny morsels of crumbled cheese and wine-soaked bits of bread. When she became lucid, he placed a pistol in her quivering hand. Between his wispy butterfly kisses and silky blackened eyelashes languorously brushing her cheek, Amelia felt immobilized in a state of suspended ecstasy. But even through this euphoric haze, his instructions permeated.

"Remain here for the night, Carina. Rest. Regain your strength. I will build a small fire. If anything -- man or animal -- threatens you, you have the gun. I will return by morning to escort you back to the town unharmed. It is one more day's trek. But first there is something I must attend to."

And then, "Ti voglio bene ogni giorno di piu`. Il mio cuore e` tutto che ti posso dare. Non ti dimentichero`.Spero che anche tu ti recorderai di me." (I love you more each day. My heart is all I have to give you. I will not forget you, I promise. I hope that you too will remember me.)

Then he was gone into the night -- like an apparition from a dreamy slumber, vanished before she could respond. Bone-weary not only by this day's flight but also by the overwhelming shock endured in the last two months, she lapsed into the deepest sleep. Sometime near dawn a shot from far above roused her, followed by another. She bolted upright, confused at first by her surroundings. Gradually her mental fuzziness abated, and she remembered – recalled everything. Tears streamed fully, copiously for her loss of this idyllic respite -- this fantastical setting where she'd been transported, as if a character in some fairy tale in which the mythical "beast" became her rescuer. No one would believe her; even she seemed uncertain where fact and fiction separated. But she was here -- scraped, scarred, bruised -- disheveled, wind-blown, and severely sunburned. It was obvious she had endured some sort of travail.

But where was he -- Eduardo? It was beyond the time of his expected arrival. And so she waited, wondering what would befall him once he'd returned her to safety.

He'd never mentioned the consequences; in fact, she had surmised everything, relying on bits of words exchanged between her captors. Her smattering of Italian might have led her to misconstrue the situation. Perhaps ransom was her own incorrect assumption -- the only hint had been the words "soldi" and "un milione." Actually, she knew nothing at all. But why was he not here by now? He was long overdue. And then something in her mind clicked -- the two shots earlier from above -- "the business" he said needed to be finished. The sun had become sweltering; she could not remain here, even though she had some water left, a bit of food, and the pistol. Her wayward heart urged her to traverse upward toward the camp where she might learn the outcome of the shots. But her head told her to continue downward toward civilization. She stood, quaking, uncertain -- and then she thought she saw a figure from high above -- she could not be sure -- she might be hallucinating in the over-powering heat. He had not seen her, but she believed she recognized the hulking, stooped, pugnacious shape. Terrified, she rapidly began her escape, trying to shield herself behind the largest boulders, gulping back her heart-rending sobs. She was in the real world now, completely on her own.

WESTWARD HO!

WESTWARD HO!

CHAPTER 1

June 28, 1876
Three days after Battle of the Little Big Horn

Sun glinted on the rugged boulders that surrounded the canyon and whose upward peaks seemed to pierce the sky. The melody of a cascading waterfall reverberated around her as White Dove knelt and cupped her hands to drink. Shafts of sunlight reflected off the silver and turquoise bracelets which cuffed her right wrist and upper arm. On her pale skin droplets of water glistened. The papoose hung lightly on her back; he was an integral part of this place since he had been conceived here. Unwinding the cord of hemp from round her waist and shoulders, she rested the sleeping child beneath a nearby bush while a gentle breeze drifted downward from the mountains, creating a windswept lullaby, as well as fanning his sweet face. The young mother dipped her hand into the water and leaning forward, extended her arm and with loving strokes, traced the features of her little son with cool, moist fingertips. He looked so much like his father -- the superbly arched eyebrows beneath a smooth, high forehead; the exceptionally long, silky eyelashes that curled gracefully upward, barely touching the prominent cheekbones; the finely chiseled nose, the flawless copper skin, the beautiful mouth. Into her memory stole that other mouth with its full and sensual lips that curled upward in a slightly mischievous smile, opening to reveal the most gleaming white and perfectly even teeth she'd ever seen. Indeed, this had been the feature that caught her attention many years ago when first she opened her eyes and saw him leaning above her. Much, much later -- it seemed eons of time later -- she came to adore that face when he reared back, his long and silky ebony mane falling around his shoulders, as he roared in delight at something that amused him. And -- much later still -- when with controlled passion he would gently take her nipple between his lips, igniting a pleasant shiver in her which would surely have remained dormant -- certainly non-existent -- if not for his patient, tender ministrations. Just the memory caused a stirring in her loins as the image of his persistent teasing tongue warmed her. When had she last known joy? Only he had succeeded in breaking through that protective barricade with which she had armored herself. Only he had been able to make her feel, to enable her to go on, to live again. It was as if he had breathed life into her, resurrecting her from the trauma that had left her dead in body and soul. She had been born again with him, named White Dove, and so had this child.

CHAPTER 2

1860

The wagon train laboriously made its way over the rugged terrain, each Conestoga dipping front-end first -- down and upward again over rocky hills and gullies, swaying side to side -- such as a boat tossed on tumultuous seas. On the seat beside her father, 'Lizbeth felt a queasiness in her stomach as the wagon shifted left to right. Beneath her the hard wooden seat seemed to splinter her skinny frame so that she felt her bones might snap in two. In his glorious descriptions of what their move West might entail, her father did not mention this physical torture. When the family had gathered at night by the blazing fire in the drafty and dilapidated old Illinois farmhouse, he would compare his own rocky, strangulated soil which resisted his repeated attempts at planting, to the rich and fertile masses of green acres awaiting them out West and free for the taking, if only they could get there. His eyes had burned with yearning, the impassioned intonation of his voice carried them as he planned the sprawling L-shaped log cabin he would build with a spacious kitchen where Mother could turn out heaps of Johnny cakes, corn muffins and apple dumplings, fruit cobblers and whatever else she fancied. The children looked up to him rapt with the vision of this abundant life, eager for him to take the final step -- sell the farm, and begin the journey. The vision of this well-built, sturdy structure set upon rolling, lushly verdant hills, with a corral of handsome, sprightly horses, and acres of corn and wheat and barley so plentiful that they could harvest from sun-up to sunset, seemed to be almost within reach. Now and then he would interrupt his narrative to ask eleven-year-old Ned where he figured the best location for the corral would be. Seven-year-old Jeremy was encouraged to build up those muscles in order to haul numerous buckets of refreshing spring water from the sparkling streams that meandered through Western valleys, even though they planned to dig a well. Father asked 'Lizbeth where she'd like to plant her garden of herbs and flowers, for even at age 14, she seemed to have a keen aesthetic sense of symmetry, proportion and form, as well as a green-thumb. Her little patch behind the barn, a small plot which she cultivated with devotion each day after chores, was a picture of delightful color with its myriad textures and shapes -- some spiked beside others softly rounded; blue delphinium behind yellow posies; orange poppies with their black-eye centers bobbing in the breeze; stark white and yellow daisies. It was here that she spent the last hours before dusk sowing, weeding, thinning and watering until she'd created an artistic masterpiece, the only bright spot in an otherwise desolate and barren property, their sole possession on this earth. 'Lizbeth noticed that Father never inquired of Mother what her preferences were for their house-to-be; and when she would steal a glance at her mother mending threadbare hand-me-downs by the scant light of the single oil-lamp, Mother did not seem to share the rapt glow and excitement on the children's faces. Rather a melancholy countenance of weary resignation hinted of broken dreams and unspoken disappointments. On this particular night if 'Lisbeth had been able to read her mother Sarah's mind, she would have known that Sarah was at least grateful that her husband was able to feed his children's imaginations, if not their bellies. Although their hunger might go unsatisfied this evening, they might be distracted with blissful dreams until morning when again they would continue their never-ending struggle to survive.

"Come along, children. Time for bed," she coaxed as she rose wearily from her chair, her back already stooped although still a young woman.

"But, Mother," protested Jeremy in his whiny child's voice, "Papa was just getting to the part where me and Ned get to go splashin' in the stream at mid-night when it's too hot to sleep inside and get to roll out blankets and bed down beneath the stars. Papa, Papa, tell us about Old Orion that will look down and wink at us from up above -- how we can talk to the stars and they will hear us. Please, Papa, please."

"Alex," Mama warned, "it's late. Growin' children need their sleep," -- "and full bellies," she thought to herself.

Sensing his wife's silent rebuke, Alex Jenks kissed each of his young-uns lovingly on the forehead and tousled their hair with a gentle hand. "Ah, my children," he crooned, "you are my beautiful creations, the fruit of my labors. If not for you..." he left unfinished the rest of his thought with a sigh of resignation.

Once the children were settled for the night and out of earshot in the cramped and drafty loft, Sarah scolded, "Why do you go fillin' their heads with fool-hearty dreams. They need to learn practical ways of dealing with reality. Ned is old enough where he could be hired out to earn his keep by harvesting crops on the Gibson's lands. And my Aunt Emily has written again offering to send fare for Elizabeth to go East for proper schoolin.' Alex, please consider these possibilities for the good of the children. We can barely feed them, and their minds and bodies waste away more each day."

"Sarah, enough! These offerings of charity are not to be accepted. I will not farm out my children, nor will I have my family separated. I have stated this before. I am their father; and with God's help and a little bit of luck, I will provide for them. It's just that we have fallen upon hard times. You must trust me and exercise some patience."

But through fifteen years of marriage and most of it a hand-to-mouth existence, Sarah's faith in her husband and patience were depleted. Their lot never seemed to improve no matter how adamantly Alex maintained his dreamy optimism and stubborn determination. In silence, she dragged herself to bed, slipped beneath what once had been a brightly patterned quilt, a wedding gift, but was now tattered and faded from much wear and many washings. Just before the much-desired oblivion of sleep rescued her, a fragment of a thought permeated her semi-consciousness -- this tattered and faded quilt was something of a symbol of her marriage. At one time upon meeting Alex Jenks and being attracted to his leprechaun charm, dazzling smile, and wildly romantic dreams, the future had appeared so bright with possibility. In their courting days as they strolled beneath beech wood trees -- their silhouettes outlined in the moonlight, he would magically weave a scenario of what their life would be, much like he had done with the children earlier tonight. In her attraction to this gentleman, who so easily made her laugh, and in her infatuation and desire to believe him, she had overlooked the most significant aspect of his personality -- that he was a dreamer who was best at planning a bright and prosperous future, but who was far from adept at accomplishing what he set out to do. Indeed, if not for the assistance from her family, they would not even have this precarious leaky roof over their heads. His dreams just never seemed to materialize; though in his own mind, he was convinced that he could bring them to fruition -- with a bit more time and luck. Like the quilt, those hopes had faded with each failed venture. Perhaps it was that he had no knack for farming. Sometimes when she observed her children attentively riveted to the fantastically entertaining tales he wove, she thought him better suited to the stage than practical living. Certainly he could enthrall an audience, as she had once been captivated by his sonorous voice, its deep inflections, the sparkling intensity of his eyes which never seemed to dull, despite repeated failures to succeed. His wild and energetic gestures still punctuated his stories with power and vitality. But gradually she had tired of his tales and dreams; they were fantasies that could not provide sustenance for her babes, wholesome food to nourish their boney, waif-like frames, or necessary medicine when they were sick. 'Lizbeth, though fourteen, had just begun her menses due to malnutrition. Now the predominant emotion Sarah experienced toward her husband was pity -- remarkable that she did not ascribe him blame for their poverty-stricken, miserable existence. Alex was certainly not a bad man; he was simply unequipped to face the real world and without the requisite practical skills of living in it. He tried -- Oh, God! -- he tried -- no one worked harder or loved his children more intensely -- which was why it was difficult to summon anger toward him. He was simply inept; and his toil and efforts ineffectual. But perhaps she too was at fault. If he had married another woman, she might have been more tolerant of his nature; and rather than always trying to curb his imagination and bring him down to earth, she might have fed his ego better. At one time as a young bride, she had felt the throes of passion beneath this quilt. In the moonlight after love-making, he would trace each of its squares, outlining the grand structure in which they someday would reside. Here would be the main house with its columned portico, stark white as this particular square. Moving his hand, he would point out the contrasting vibrant red square next to it where she could grow the velvety red roses whose scent she so adored. Here a patterned green square represented acres of rolling lawns surrounding the stately residence, and on and on until she would close her eyes, and their future home would appear before her in all its glorious detail. She would be lulled to sleep with those rosy dreams of the future. Now after fifteen hard laborious years and numerous disappointments, the quilt's squares were dulled as were the images in her head. At least in these fifteen years he had reined in his ambitious fantasizing to a more reasonable scale; the grand edifice had diminished, to a leak-proof cabin. Yet still she never hated him, not even now as her stomach growled with hunger, her back ached severely from fatigue and hours walking behind the plow sowing seeds in the pebbly dirt that never seemed to produce the expected and longed-for crop. A faint stirring in her belly heightened her alarm, as she wondered if that foreshadowed the arrival of another mouth to feed. When her husband reached for her beneath the heavy quilt, groping for her breast in the darkened room, the last vestige of hope and energy deserted her, and she pretended to be deeply asleep.

CHAPTER 3

Now en route across the Western Plains, "The Promised Land," the wagon rumbled forward on rickety wheels, dipping and rolling, doggedly forced by the sheer determination and desperation of Alex Jenks. By his side sat 'Lizbeth, a rifle in her hands. Ned and Jeremy limped with fatigue and thirst beside the over-taxed animals, while Sarah lay feverish and racked with pain in the back of the Conestoga. Occasionally she would be blessed with a brief respite from her agony, as God would bless her with a few moments of sweet oblivion. She yearned to be free of this suffering; for it at last to be over. In one of those fleeting reveries, she pictured herself ensconced in the comfortable, commodious home that Alex had promised them. Another time she hallucinated that they had finally reached their destination -- a fertile valley with lush, rolling green expanse; but these fantasies would be obliterated by the searing hot stabs of pain shooting through her abdomen; and in her last lucid moments, she did not believe that she would ever see it in this life. A wet stickiness beneath her told her that she was bleeding profusely -- perhaps hemorrhaging -- and there was a rhythmic persistent drumming in her temples. This pounding in her head was assuaged only by her drifting in and out of consciousness. In another quickly fleeting dream she remembered the event that brought them to this point -- their sorry, pitiful cabin ablaze, flames whipping their nightclothes, singeing their shins, acrid smoke filling their lungs, choking cries from the children as they frantically sought escape from the smothering fog. Unbelievably, but fortunately, all had escaped with varying degrees of minor burns and smoke inhalation; but all had survived, with the exception of their dwelling. In the horror of the moment and the dwelling's pitiable state, it didn't seem a great loss. In fact, after the initial shock and subsequent relief to be actually cradling his beloved children in his arms, Alex Jenks was able to take even this dismal tragedy, the demise of their one possession on earth, and turn it into a fortuitous event. Now there was no reason to remain here. At last they could fulfill his long-delayed dream of finding new opportunity out West. Alex had been eagerly waiting the imminent passage of "The Homestead Act" that promised every household 160 acres in Kansas and Nebraska, free for the taking. He was itching even before that when gold had been discovered in California in 1848 and then again in 1859 in The Black Hills of South Dakota. He had missed so many opportunities. This was his last chance; he was no longer a young man. The tear-stained, smutty cheeks of the children soon shone with optimistic smiles, as beneath the stars their father did again what he did so well -- weave hauntingly beautiful plans to quell their fear and lull them into fantastical expectations.

CHAPTER 4

In between her sporadic spasms and delirium, Sarah Jenks sensed that they had increased their speed. Indeed, it was the dervish swaying of the second-hand wagon that exacerbated her excruciating pain, and now she howled in agony. What she could not comprehend was why no one -- neither her husband nor the children -- addressed her anguished cries. Perhaps they had hastened their speed in a frenzied attempt to catch up to the wagon train from which they had been temporarily separated while Alex repaired a broken axle. He had assured them they would be within the protective ring of the circled wagons before dusk, but the repair had taken longer than anticipated as he labored clumsily with the tools at his disposal. The wagon itself was is poor shape when Alex purchased it, but it was all he could afford and was eager to start the journey. When Sarah initially saw it, her heart sank as her instincts told her that this conveyance was not prairie-worthy. Theirs would be a tortuous trip over parched deserts, rugged steep mountains, and treacherous swirling streams. But what choice did she have? There was no place to return to; they could only go forward. As usual, Alex had tried to allay their apprehension and alleviate their recent trauma by spinning yarns about the future that awaited them beyond this challenging terrain. As she had since the day she met him, she followed his lead. What alternative did she have?

Alex was following the path made by former wagon trains, clearly delineated by two lines of sunflowers that had grown in the ruts created by their wheels. In what would be her final reverie, Sarah thought death had finally released her into blissful, heavenly peace for which she was so earnestly praying. But instead looming before her face appeared a grotesquely painted monster, the heat of his breath upon her cheek, streaks of crimson paint slashed upon the sides of his face from upper cheeks to lower jaws. A grisly scar ran vertically down the right side of his forehead severing his right eyebrow, so that it appeared to be cut in half. It was her last image, as with a ferocious, blood-curdling screech from his snarled lips, he buried the tomahawk he had been wielding above the semi-conscious Sarah into her perspiring prow. Both blood and sweat mingled in a profuse outpouring of life.

From her precarious perch beside her father, 'Lizbeth turned just in time to see this bloody spectacle of horror. She had dropped the rifle as she clutched with both hands the wooden seat beneath her in a frantic attempt to avoid being thrown from the tottering wagon. Mercilessly her father whipped the staggering animals in a futile attempt to escape the yelping warriors who pursued them. In utter helplessness, 'Lizbeth saw her little brother Jeremy trampled beneath hooves and wheels as he desperately tried to clamber up to the violently swerving wagon. As for Ned, in the frenzy and terror of the moment, she'd lost sight of him. When she'd turned to see the savage desecration of her mother, her brother had vanished into nothingness. Behind her, the interior of the wagon appeared bathed in a continuing sea of red. Her mother's still and lifeless form lay swimming in blood. In a split second she saw the painted creature pull his hatchet from Sarah's split skull and heft it forward toward her father's back. Through the canvas opening at the wagon's rear, she saw other savages in wild pursuit. She squeezed her eyes shut and lost consciousness.

CHAPTER 5

Lizbeth lay on her back, legs spread-eagled, buried in some nightmarish miasma in which she lay drowning. Gulping and gasping for air, it felt as if she were being smothered by some ponderous weight crushing against her chest and some knife-like, piercing pressure between her legs. In her semi-conscious state, she was suspended from reality. In a dazed stupor, her vacant, hollowed eyes beheld that same streaked and painted face with the scarred eyebrow lolling above and close to her own. It was the evil visage of her mother's assailant. In an effort to rid herself of the sight of his odious, wildly contorted countenance, she turned her head aside only to see another savage wielding a sharp-bladed knife in one hand and in the other yanking upward the full and wavy hair of her nearly lifeless father. With one deft stroke from the back of the crown to the front, he swiftly lifted the top skin of her father's scalp and slashed it upward. Again he brought the knife down twice in single swoops, severing both ears as blood gushed from both sides of her father's head. His heart-rending, shrill scream pierced her semi-conscious state, mixed with a guttural yelp choked from the deepest part of her rapist. With this strangled sound, his rhythmic plunging inside her ceased. Turning her head away in the opposite direction she saw two young bucks with Ned dangling between them. The one on the left had Ned's left hand and foot while the one on the right held her brother's right hand and foot. Together they raised and swung him three times, turning him loose on the third swing. Cutting a somersault in the air, he hit the ground, a mangled corpse. Immediately, a dog came running to lap up the blood oozing from Ned's lethal wounds -- his fine fair hair blowing in the breeze. She opened her mouth in a helpless, outraged cry of protestation for the devastating loss of her loved-ones as well as of her innocence; but her scream was soundless, as if she too had perished along with her family around her. Yanking up the leggings worn beneath his breechcloth, the satiated savage strode away.

CHAPTER 6

Black Elk found her nearly two days later lying partially submerged in a stream some distance from the site of the hideous family massacre. From her tracks, he concluded that she had wandered aimlessly before collapsing here. He held her limp body in his arms, cooling her sunburnt brow and arms with water from the stream. Lifting the girl's frail body, he carried her gently to a softly woven blanket placed beneath the shade of an out-spreading bush. Unaware, she listlessly reclined there, as he made a small fire, gathered some chokecherries which he crushed in a small amount of water and heated it upon the fire. Then cutting leaves from an aloe bush, the Indian slashed them in the center and suspended them in the sun, points downward to drip into small containers. With this colorless liquid, he mixed mud to make an ointment-poultice and applied it to her bruised and battered body. As he ministered to her, he was fascinated by everything about her -- the porcelain skin, the delicate limbs, and long silky strands of hair the color of golden wheat. Her graceful neck resembled that of a swan; and he was mesmerized by this most exquisite creature, unlike any person he had ever seen before. Sitting behind her, he placed her head in his lap, raising it as he pinched the lips slightly to open them. In his left hand he held her up-turned chin while with his right he worked her mouth to take in the therapeutic, medicinal brew, drop by drop. Her eyes flitted open for just a second, and Black Elk's heart quickened. Their purity and wild-flower blue color penetrated his very soul so that he felt an unaccustomed quavering in his body. He yearned to see her open them again, if only for a second. He felt her pulse which now was becoming steadier and every so-slightly stronger. These sensations unnerved him. From young boyhood he had heard male warriors of his tribe describe these indications of female attraction, but these were unfamiliar and unsettling. It was not only her exotic, unique coloring which would certainly be a curiosity in this area; but also a protective instinct from deep within made him want to shield this bird-like creature from this harsh environment to which she was so ill-equipped in stature and constitution. As he scooped small sips of liquid between her even teeth he studied the soft curve of her lips beneath a small, pert nose. Even the tiny ear-lobes seemed perfectly proportioned to her flawless, sweet face. He saw that she was not quite yet a woman. Absorbing all this, he knew that by the laws of his tribe, a warrior could take a captive as his bride and was expected to become responsible for her. One who was considered unsuitable or a burden to sustain -- particularly in harsh winters or seasons of famine -- would be given up for torture to the women of the tribe. But he had no intention of abandoning her, although he knew that her unusual beauty would foster resentment and jealousy among the females. Some would consider her alien and too fragile to sufficiently contribute to the community -- to carry her own weight without being a burden to others. If such was to be her lot, better to leave her here to die. But he knew even as he considered her slim chances of survival in the harsh Indian way of life, that already she exuded a *naglia*, a certain essence that tugged at the innermost depths of his soul, as well as a *sicun,* a power that he was unable to resist. His father, the shaman of the tribe, had told him it would be like this someday with the woman for whom he was destined; a man was not complete without this soulmate. Until now those had merely been words he did not comprehend. He wondered if his instincts were reliable. How could one so foreign captivate him so completely? In his world it was dangerous to lose control of one's emotions. But even so, his father had foretold that when one found his other half intended by the Great Sprit, it would render him stronger; for two halves comprise the whole. Lost in his musings, he did not see at first the blue eyes flicker, then open to look backwards and upwards into his. Although the eyes were the soft hue of delphiniums, they seemed lifeless and shrouded with a death-like haze. He was not certain that she saw him, although her eyes were wide open. This child-woman gazed up at him with the vacant eyes of the old blind Indian whose eternal stare was empty and unknowing. Black Elk felt a wave of pain contract his entire being, for surely her *niya* (spirit of vitality that sustains life) was gone. The *iya* (master of all malevolence) may have spared her body, but not her soul. Nevertheless, he had found her, so she was his, broken as she was. He would take her back with him; he could not -- would not -- relinquish her now, convinced as he was that he had found in her that essential piece that would make him whole. With patience and tenderness, he would rejuvenate her spirit. It must be so or he would remain forever half alive. He did not know how he knew this; but he knew that it was so. She with him together would endure.

CHAPTER 7

And so 'Lizbeth came into the tribe as White Dove, the name bestowed upon her by Black Elk. Technically by Indian law, she was his captive. At first she was an object of curiosity with her strange, pale coloring, long flowing flaxen hair, wraithlike appearance, and cornflower blue eyes. But more arresting than the unique color of her eyes was their wild, vacant gaze that was a cause of wonder. She seemed to look outward and beyond, oblivious to all around her. Those unusual eyes appeared totally unfocused on any specific object or person. Whether lying in the tipi of Black Elk's family where she was first brought to rest and recuperate, or later when she gained the strength to be incorporated into the labors of the women, those eyes never lost their lifeless glaze. Nor did White Dove utter any word or sound. Working beside the other females, she gathered wild roots and berries, wove baskets and blankets, smoked and dried meat for jerky. It was almost as if she neither wanted to see nor speak. Black Elk's mother was kind and patient with her, sensing that this silence had not always been the case, although others speculated that this white girl might have been mute from birth. Her hands moved in silent labor, but her countenance and body movements showed no expression. With stoical acceptance, she endured fatigue, discomfort, hunger, cold -- winter temperatures could drop to 40 degrees below. Because she withstood all bravely and silently, she became an object of wonder even to Indians, schooled from birth to deprivation. Not only did this wild and vacant look distinguish her, but also her total silence. She never made a human sound -- not sigh nor sob nor laugh. Despite this lack of communication with others, no one shunned her. Only Black Elk's mother, called "Great Mother," had any human communion with her since it was necessary that she teach White Dove how to crush the corn for meal; how to prepare cords for fishing and to extract oil from the fish once caught; how to skin the freshly killed rabbit, raccoons, beavers, and muskrats; and how to string and sew the beads onto clothing. Sometimes together, they would venture into the woods in search of *chanakpa (big mushrooms)* growing in elm trees. With sticks, they'd knock them down, gather them, coat them with flour and fry them for Black Elk's favorite dish. *Wasna`* (jerky) was another favorite. They scraped pieces from the animal hide, which then they pounded and dried; mixed with melted fat, sugar, and dried fruit, it made a tasty food. In addition, she was instructed in the work of treating bison skins for tipis; the construction of each required ten or more hides; then she learned to weave mats for sleeping. Great Mother would gently touch her forearm, take her hand, and demonstrate the proper motions to complete the assigned work. From dawn until dusk, the women were endlessly busy. From a distance, Black Elk would look, observing White Dove cocooned in this shell of isolation with which she had enveloped herself. He did not believe it was by choice. His heart ached for her pain and his own loneliness. Until he could make her his, he remained as half alive as she. Recalling White Dove's condition when first he found her, he was aware of her trauma at the hands of some other tribe. This territory and its environs was inhabited by Crow, Cheyenne, Arapaho, as well Dakota Sioux. From his own wikiup at night, unable to sleep, he looked across to where she slept in the tipi of Great Mother and his father, as the long hours dragged until dawn.

Another fact that aroused curiosity among the females was that there was never a need each month for her to join the menstruating women in the tiny segregated huts at the edge of the encampment which was the custom. There for four days these women rested from their labors. Such segregation was considered necessary so as to not defile sacred objects or contaminate war weapons which then might bring harm to the warriors, particularly before battle. Only Black Elk knew for certain why this was so; and soon Great Mother sensed as well when White Dove's thin and boney fame began to take on a rounded quality. Her pert and tiny breasts began to swell beneath her deerskin dress, as did her abdomen beneath its fringed yoke. Even this condition -- *owewah* (with child) -- she did not acknowledge in any manner. Without abatement, she continued with her chores beside Great Mother until she was so bloated and full-bellied that she could no longer stoop to gather wild berries and seeds or carry the heavy containers filled with water from the stream. Still she would valiantly attempt to complete these expected tasks, until Great Mother would take her hand and lead her into the shade of the tipi where she would stroke her arms, then her back, or even cradle her in her arms and sing a lullaby. Great Mother sensed that this child-woman was innocent regarding her pregnancy, although it had never been discussed with her son. She knew too that Black Elk was entranced with this girl, so she did for White Dove all she could. She had come not only admire the girl's fortitude but had also begun to feel a deep affection. Her vulnerability touched the older woman's heart which ached for the defilement of the girl's body and what she surmised had caused the silence. Although Great Mother attempted in many ways to demonstrate her growing fondness, all attempts went unrewarded. Never once did White Dove smile or look warmly into her eyes. She appeared inured to any overt display of emotion.

No one living, not even White Dove herself, was aware that she had passed her 15th birthday. And then, in the ninth month following her arrival, Great Mother was awakened in the wee hours before dawn by restless movement on the other side of the tipi. The soon-to-be-mother lay on her back, her knees raised as she writhed to left and right. Great Mother had witnessed many births, but never one like this of uncanny silence. Approaching the pregnant girl, the older woman placed her hand upon the swollen abdomen, just as a sudden gush of water emerged from between the raised legs. Her husband gathered his blanket and went to their son's wikiup as it was not considered proper for males to observe childbirth; but it was empty. When Black Elk had seen the firelight from his parents' tent, he was on his way. He had kept vigil through the night since his mother had predicted that birth was imminent. He did not care that a male should not be in attendance and immediately positioned himself behind White Dove so as to hold her in a sitting position against his chest, stroking her arms as his mother applied cold compresses to her forehead in an attempt to soothe her silent agony. Yellow wisps of hair curled in damp ringlets around her ashen face, and the beads of perspiration on her forehead glistened in the firelight. The only sound to emerge from her was a rhythmic panting and heaving. Great mother prepared the boiling water, took a newly woven pristine blanket, stacked stones upon the fire needed for warming the newborn. Black Elk coaxed her labor with comforting words, blowing breath upon his beloved's cheeks to cool her. Finally, Great Mother instructed him to carry White Dove to a holding rod which had been designed some weeks ago for this very purpose. Before this horizontal piece of wood, suspended between two-foot bars, he positioned her, placing her hands in a grip upon the bar. Kneeling behind her squatting body, he took its weight against his own, straining in sync with her every exertion to push. Almost as one, he would feel the pressure in her pelvis rise, then fall, then rise again. The swell just above her pubic area seemed to move forward, then recede again and again. It seemed as if the weight of this moving mound could crush her delicate frame. Her silent agony was torture for Black Elk to watch. He felt compelled to be her voice, screaming her pain and outrage for this defilement upon her delicate body. But he did not. Something deep within her had been silenced, perhaps because her cries of wild terror and protest had gone unheeded during the assault that resulted in this pregnancy. Observing her son's contorted countenance, Great Mother took pride in his true Lakota heart since they believed that emotions are what made one thrive and experience life in full measure. But this also engendered her fear, since a Sioux warrior was taught from boyhood to keep emotions in tight control, to maintain an expressionless countenance that hid all feelings. Of course, this was a necessary tool when dealing with the enemy whom you didn't want to "read" your face. A stone-like visage was conducive for survival. One's thoughts must be indecipherable; to do otherwise was to reveal weakness. Both she and her husband had been concerned about their son's open and affectionate nature since childhood. They had made both subtle and overt attempts to reshape this trait, not only for his own protection but also to insure acceptance by the tribe. She even doubled the hides of panther upon which he slept at night, for it was believed a child would absorb the qualities of the animal that made his mattress. Girls slept on fawn skins. Sioux males were expected to camouflage their warmer feelings under the guise of indifference. Perhaps White Dove was better at this guise than Black Elk, and perhaps that was part of the awe in which she was looked upon by male and female tribe members alike. She displayed nothing. But in the matter of this woman, her son was incapable of demonstrating indifference -- quite the contrary. Good that there was no one here to witness what they might judge unmanly. Although in private they were playful and affectionate, Indians were expected to appear sphinxlike, even after long separations; when returning, they would not jubilantly run to each other and embrace as they would love to; but rather they would be expected to respond with an impassive stare which had been very difficult to inculcate in her son as a young boy. He was an anomaly in this culture. If anything, joy was "written all over his face;" and he had to be conditioned to shed these open-faced tendencies. Great Mother loathed to use punishment as did other mothers who scratched the child's legs with sharp switches, deeply enough to draw blood, in order to bring about the desired behavior. But she did not; perhaps she herself was an anomaly as well.

Never had a male participated in the birth process; and it was almost as if White Dove sensed this, for she stifled all cries that might bring attention to her plight. Eventually spent and exhausted, she relinquished her grip on the rod and fell against Black Elk's *haska* (long and lean frame). He steadied her, covered her hands with his own, and placed them again upon the rod, gripping it along with her. Again moving together in rhythm as one body, despite searing pain ripping her apart, both he and Great Mother finally saw the tiny infant drop from his mother's womb. It was only at that moment that mother and son saw two silent single tears from White Dove's eyes before she fell into exhausted oblivion. Great Mother hoped those tears indicated some dormant remnant of emotion still alive within the deepest recesses of this girl's soul. On those two tears, Black Elk would pin his hopes for her return to life and the living.

CHAPTER 8

When White Dove finally awakened from her exhausting labor, she was no longer *owewha* (a woman with child). The odious presence that had so weighted her down and contorted her tiny frame was gone, but it had been replaced by an overwhelming emptiness. Her formerly pain-wracked pelvis -- indeed her entire assaulted body -- felt like a void. Turning her head that was resting upon a reed-filled thrush pillow, she saw Great Mother by the firelight in deep contemplation. White Dove had slept while Great Mother performed the ablutions upon the male newborn -- plunging him four times in cold water as was their custom -- massaging his limbs, then swaddling him in a softly woven blanket, after disposing of the after-birth. But as she tended the infant, she had been arrested by his eyes which unsettled her. Many moons ago, when she was being trained in the art of midwifery, the aged crone instructor who had the experience of many seasons, said that the true soul of a newborn was reflected in his eyes. They revealed his *nagi* (personality) and his *nagila* (essence). When Black Elk had been born and placed in Great Mother's arms, his eyes possessed a shiny clarity. As she caressed his dimpled cheeks, those eyes reflected *si-cun* (powers of good); this child, she knew then, would be a blessing; and such had indeed proved true. But White Dove's infant had small, deeply set, jet-black eyes, piercing in their gaze. Although she knew that babies could not see immediately at birth so that to him she was only a shadow, even in this incipient stage, she felt those penetrating eyes foretold something ominous -- although intangible, nearly pal-pable. As she handled the baby, she seemed an unwilling captive to his stone countenance; and she was reminded of *Iwa*, the master of all malevolence, whose breath brought disease and tragedy to all who encountered this force. With an involuntary shiver, she placed the child in the cradle-board made by her son. Its wooden frame was wrapped in soft brown deerskin, which had been flayed and tanned by Great Mother and White Dove, although the mother-to-be did not know that these would hold her babe. Such preparation of hides was a long and laborious process done by females, although Black Elk had hunted for these hides himself and reserved them for this purpose. They had been washed, scraped, and left to soak in water for three days to soften them. They would be used to cover the frame of cedar wood, which Black Elk cut and smoothed, then lined the cradle-board with moss and cattail down, both well-dried so as to provide comfort and also serve as an absorbent, disposable diaper. In addition, he had fashioned a wooden bow which projected from the top and to this, he'd hung a piece of fabric to protect from sun and insects. At the bottom was a small shelf on which the tiny feet would rest. From the sinewy laces that held the baby in place dangled colorful beads he had woven into bands of geometrical design. Finally, it had been smoked and blessed with sage. Although it was frowned upon to start a cradle before the baby's birth, Black Elk considered this case an exception. He had also fashioned adorable baby moccasins, embellished with miniature glass seed beads of pink, light blue, and lavender set in circle and triangle shapes. The crafting of a cradle was considered an act of love. The meticulous care which Black Elk had devoted to fashioning it concerned his mother; for she knew that according to the tribal laws, although captives might be adopted into their midst, *iyeska* (half-breed child) could never be accepted.

Cradles physically and symbolically represented closeness in family, especially through generations, and this child was not one of theirs. The lattice cradle was designed to be worn on the mother's back at eye-level with adults who could stimulate with frequent eye and voice contact. In that way an infant, cozy and safe attached to its mother, was socialized, gaining immediate sense that they were part of a tribal community; but White Dove would not be carrying her baby in this manner. So Great Mother was not surprised, that once the preparation was complete, Black Elk lifted infant and cradle and in great strides exited the tipi. She did not know his intentions.

Great Mother turned toward White Dove, still unconscious, her wan and pallid face drained of all energy. She wondered what White Dove had felt, if anything -- all these months with the fetus resting beneath her breasts, stirring against her ribs. She had merely been the receptacle for the red-man's seed, a cavity for the alien presence. The pregnancy was the result of the assault upon the young girl's innocence and virginity -- Great Mother was certain -- an assault so psychically damaging that she no longer could give voice to it. That attack and whatever horror she'd witnessed had silenced her as completely as a cork plugs up the neck of a bottle. It was best White Dove would be spared those eyes that would pierce her very soul, just as its father had penetrated her body. In Black Elk's tribe such an aggressor would have been made to run the gauntlet receiving heavy, violent blows and kicks from left and right, a beating by his tribesmen leaving him a bloody pulp. In addition, it was likely he'd have the tip of his nose cut off, or, at the very least, his nostrils slit. Then, worst of all, he would be exiled from their midst, a roving outcast for evermore; for a brave without a tribe was like a man without a country. But in this case the defiler had escaped with impunity since his identity was unknown.

CHAPTER 9

The vanilla white moon shone upon the silhouette of a majestic brave on horseback carrying this *iyeska*. Gingerly the horse made its way over rocky terrain. Gigantic, stalagmite boulders pierced the violet sky that appears soon before dawn. Black Elk loved this beautiful high country and its wild inhabitants -- deer, mountain lions, bears, and bobcats. His was a spiritual connection to the land, as was the case with all Indians. Most would have abandoned this child to the wilderness beyond the Minneconjou Crossing, to the fangs of wolves and coyotes; but this babe was a part of her. In fact, except for those intensely ebony eyes and lightly bronze skin-tone, this child did not have predominantly ethnic Native American features. The slight peach-fuzz of hair was of a sandy hue, indicating inheritance from his mother's side. He was an odd mixture -- neither Indian nor completely Caucasian.

For many months in anticipation of this responsibility, Black Elk had searched for what he sensed was the "right" place. He had visited much territory beyond the Black Hills and had reached his decision and destination -- a moderately-sized homestead at the western edge of the canyon. In its center was a sturdy log-cabin, smoke swirling upward from its stone chimney. Colorfully printed calico curtains had been drawn across the windows against the chilly drafts of the night air. In the rear, the owner was attempting to coax an assortment of wildflowers from the parched earth. And further back beneath a grassy knoll was a small fenced in area enclosing three small headstones: Davey (age 6), "First-born Son of Charles and Emma Reynolds;" Emily Reynolds (age 2), "Beloved Daughter"); and Betsy Reynolds (stillborn) "With the Angels." In front of each was a container of withered flowers; but Black Elk knew from past visits, that after completing household chores and assisting her husband in plowing and sowing in the fields, the woman would come here to replace the dying flowers with fresh ones. Then she would kneel at each grave, her head bowed, her lips moving, before kissing her fingertips and lovingly touching the ground where each child lay. Then sitting off to the right side, with a book open in her lap, she would read aloud. From one tome, he knew to be the White Man's prayer book -- large, black, and leather-bound -- she would read in a soothing, melodious soft voice. The other she read with animated expression, as if weaving tales of magic and mystery for her children -- reading to them as if they were alive to listen. Then at the end she would stare silently -- her tears dampening the earth -- before she would rise and dejectedly return to her empty dwelling. Black Elk did not know the words she uttered in this daily ritual, but what he DID know was that this grieving mother would welcome and accept the infant in his arms. The warrior surmised that this cabin had once housed those dead children as there was a wide-planked porch on which no children played now. Nevertheless, a weathered cradle still swayed to and fro in the pre-dawn breeze, as if someone had forgotten to bring it indoors or could not bear to remove it. He had seen no son laboring in the fields beside his father. From his frequent observations over nine-months' time, he sensed intuitively that White Dove's infant would occupy this carefully carved, hand-made cradle, once freshly painted; and that a baby would fill this grieving woman's arms with solace -- would be rocked and sung-to, cuddled and kissed. This child, although denied a place by the laws of the Indians, would be embraced by a woman more capable than its own fragile mother. This was the baby's best chance. Black Elk had deeply pondered all possibilities before mak-ing this decision. Looking upward, he prayed for this child's welfare to the Morning Star which appears just before dawn. It was the belief of his people that if one prayed at this moment, the wish expressed in the prayers would come to fruition. And so creeping stealthily beneath the auspicious Star, he placed the sleeping child in the rock-ing cradle.

CHAPTER 10

Black Elk did not immediately return to his village. In the pre-dawn purple light, he searched diligently through the forest for a particular wild root believed to have magical healing powers for a troubled spirit. Along the path, he easily found various nuts, berries, and acorns, but this particular root with supposed medicinal psychological powers eluded him. As he observed White Dove's entirely passive demeanor these past nine months, as well as the forlorn vacancy in her face, he vowed that if it took his entire lifetime, he would make up to her for what she so silently suffered. It would be his mission to rekindle the light that had been extinguished in her soul. Each time he attempted to make eye contact with those eternally downcast liquid blue pools, his heart rent in his chest in tenderness and pity. When often he felt this, he associated it with his boyhood experiences discovering a small, helpless, in-jured animal that he would scoop up, lavishing upon it reassuring, gentle strokes to calm its terrified yelps. How he yearned to do the same for her, but it had taken extreme willpower to not touch her.

Although his tribesmen frowned upon overtly demonstrative gestures toward their women and considered them unmanly, Black Elk marched "to his own drummer" and had sufficiently demonstrated in battle and elsewhere that he was an able warrior worthy of respect and admiration. When he was growing up, Great Mother had been concerned that his sensitive and softer nature would make him the object of taunts and teasing. In concern for his standing within the tribe, she had forced herself to relinquish signs of affection so as to toughen him up. Her heart ached to run to him when he struggled or stumbled, but she held herself in check. One day when only six, he had been unseated and thrown violently from a pony. Her husband had warned her not to encourage this child's innate sensitivity, but this was different. He could be severely injured which had nothing to do with his gentle nature. Those who were indeed effeminate (*berdaches*) were made to inhabit the area on the outskirts of the camp where they dressed as women and performed chores assigned to females, although their homosexuality carried no stigma. But as her son matured, his considerate nature concerned her less and less as he became the epitome of masculine appeal -- broad-shouldered, lean frame, sinewy muscles rippling beneath flawless bronzed skin, a thick black mane framing a ruggedly handsome visage -- inspiring awe and respect from all. Even that quiet, pensive nature she had so often fretted about, became an asset. Without ego, he never became embroiled in argument or competition so that he never offended anyone, nor harbored any begrudging foes. He was a man to be reckoned with and no one questioned his strength or bravery; his was a formidable, arresting presence -- a fine figure whether astride a horse or standing on the ground. His speech was calm and deliberate, his demeanor dignified. He exuded confidence. Although he was the object of admiring glances from the single females, he had given his heart to no one -- until now. Great Mother knew her son -- adored him with every ounce of her being -- and believed that it was not only his noble stature that attracted them but also the kind softness in his eyes --so very rare in their culture. Boys were conditioned through childhood, to be tough; and Black Elk demonstrated that he could hold his own from very young. When at 12, like all pre-teens, he was sent off for a month alone into the wilderness on a hunting expedition required to demonstrate survival skills, he had returned proudly with a multitude of bloody prey -- rabbits, beaver, coons, and muskrat -- dangling from his spear. He had even crowned himself with horns from an antelope he slew, and told of his cunning maneuvers to escape a bear attack, as well as encounters with bob-cats and a mountain lion. Later he would be awarded many eagle feathers in a "counting coup" for his brave deeds. Even as a participant in boyhood games intended as training for endurance in with-standing pain, he had never flinched when the core of the sunflower was placed upon his arm and lit with fire. Great Mother had come to realize that her concerns had been needless; the son of whom she was so proud and loved so dearly, was more than adequately fit to pass any test of manhood. She had sensed he was what the Kiowa tribe called *auday* (specially favored), blessed to grow up with a greater sense of responsibility toward others -- one who represented the most ideal qualities. Indeed, he was maturing to be the epitome of a fine Lakota brave with an abundance of their most valued traits: bravery, integrity, honesty, and generosity. He would mature to become an awesome specimen of masculinity, much like the esteemed chief Red Cloud, who although brave and courageous, demonstrated a kind and gentle nature.

CHAPTER 11

Black Elk took his time returning to his village some distance away. He loved this grand landscape, especially at this hour -- beautiful high country hills dotted with pinion, cedar, and juniper trees. In summer it was covered with multi-colored wildflowers, as if painted with an Indian paint brush. These were punctuated by cacti, cholla, and tall sage. Black Elk swept his eyes across the horizon where piles of rotting buffalo were strewn across the prairies. He deplored this wasteful slaughter of the buffalo on which his people relied for survival. What would be their food source in the coming months? What skins would provide clothing and shelter? Filled with anger, he resented that the US government encouraged more and more white settlers to come to this region; it was a deliberate attempt to make Indian life difficult, to curtail their food supply by exterminating the buffalo and coercing the Indians to become dependent, subject to the white man's mercy. He was aware that the youngest of the "invaders" had formed hunting groups on horseback to "have fun" attacking the buffalo, which were even targets of sport for bored and weary travelers looking for diversion who aimed at them from moving railroad cars. Black Elk had heard of the despicable "Bill Cody," who boasted that he alone had killed 4,280 buffalo in 7 months. He had been a meat hunter for the Goddard Brothers who fed the construction crews of the Kansas-Pacific Railroad. On the plains one could see him in his fringed buckskins, long blond hair and trimmed goatee, cutting a handsome figure; but he was known to drink as much as two quarts of liquor a day. Black Elk had heard that the most prominent spokesman for the US government was quoted in the newspaper of the pale-faces as saying that "These white hunters have done more to settle the vexing Indian question than the entire army has done in 30 years. For the sake of lasting peace, let them kill, skin, and sell until the buffalo are exterminated." Such words aroused such bitter rage, he feared for the intended destruction of his people and their way of life. Buffalo were easy sport since they had poor eyesight and an entire herd could be killed while they grazed one by one. Recently, he had attended many councils where Sioux Chief Sitting Bull had been visited by delegates from other Plains tribes, often their competitors, but in this mutual threat, were joining forces against annihilation of them all. At the center of these gatherings, Lakota Chief Crazy Horse reminded them of "their rightful place in the Universe given to them by the Great Spirit (the Master of Life) and the sacred obligations to the cosmos" that accompanied that gift. They could not possibly exist outside this land because they had come FROM it and were a PART of it.

At this assembly of tribes, the Chief's voice had proclaimed: "The white man does not have the land in his soul or its dust in his bones. He wants only to rape it and bleed it dry. One does not sell the land on which the people walk. They do not see that the treasure in this land is NOT the gold they seek, but in the power of the SPIRIT that is its very essence. Without land we are nothing!"

Chief White Bull had spoken in the same vein: "Mother Nature provides for us all we need, but the White Men have disrupted the balance and ruined our Paradise made by *Thunkashila* (The Creator). They have not only slaughtered the buffalo, leaving them to rot on the plains, but have also felled our forests so that there is no game to hunt. Our children are starving and die while their mothers' cries are carried on the night wind. Our history is written on the four winds. If we surrender our land as they demand, we surrender our very souls and the lives of our children. THE LAND IS OUR SACRED OBLIGATION, OUR BLOOD, AND OUR FUTURE. TAKE OUR LAND AWAY AND WE DIE."

Mary Brave Bird: "They label us 'hostiles' when all we want is to be left alone on land that is ours. They offer our land freely to the prospectors and settlers who do not respect it. We want to keep what is ours, the rich and fertile ground of our ancestors. *Maka ke wakan* (the land is sacred). It is our mother. We have an umbilical cord tying us to the land. The universe is our family. Brother Moon watches over us at night. Sister Sun warms us in the day. We need to feel the prairie wind upon our face with its scent of sage and sweet grass."

Chief Gall: "First prospectors came to our Black Hills in 1859, looking for gold. The Black Hills is *Paha Sapa* (sacred land) -- not only sacred, but beautiful -- majestic mountains, sparkling lakes, pine-covered rolling hills, towers of granite that soar up to the sky. There is no price to equal this beauty. "Lonesome" Charley Reynolds tell his "big Boss Custer" that a miner can earn $150 in white man's money each day. From Ft. Laramie they send news by "wire" they call telegraph. This news they write in Eastern newspaper, and then they come in droves."

"We -- Sioux, Cheyenne, Arapaho -- took action -- attacked white trespassers, for that is what they are. We destroyed their government forts. Then "Homestead Act" in 1862-- this time they come for land -- each homesteader/160 acres -- OUR land United States government STEALS from us and gives to THEM. Five years later, they start the railroad and build Bozeman's Trail (1867) to gold fields in Montana. They should call it 'thieves' road.' Their steam trains frighten away the buffalo, disturb our livestock, damage our crops. It is not enough that we tear up the tracks and put huge logs to derail the 'iron horse.' They still keep coming and want to move us onto reservations. We KNOW OUR RIGHTFUL PLACE in *oyate* (universe) and IT IS HERE! The bones of our ancestors are buried in that earth. White men do not share our reverence for the land. They plunder it with no thought of the future. What will be left when they are finished?"

Little Chief of the Cheyennes rose and bellowed: "There will be NO MORE TREATIES! We have a long history with them of broken treaties. Remember Harney Sandborn Treaty -- 1866. Remember 1868 -- Treaty of Ft. Laramie -- they promised that forever The Black Hills were for our use alone -- white men forbidden to enter. Ha! And did they keep their promise? Crazy Horse was right to refuse to sign the treaty. We have been cheated again and again. We wanted no war with the 'White Knives,' but they have forced us."

Then rose Red Cloud, leader of the Oglala Lakota, a branch of the Teton Sioux, the bravest of all the Sioux. As a young boy he had fought against neighboring Pawnee and Crow, gaining much experience in warfare. At the early age of 35, he had already risen to a tribal leader -- strong, brave, a bold rider and splendid horseman, expert in weaponry. In addition, he had swum across both the Missouri and Yellowstone Rivers, his courage unquestionable and his bearing dignified. He had listened to all, considered their statements, as was always the case with chiefs of the Plains Indians. More democratic than most, no chief truly had supreme power; rather they took the advice of others under consideration before meeting in pow-wow (council) to decide on a course of action.

"Friends and brothers, listen to my words. Those before me speak the truth. WE are a great and powerful people who are being driven from our rightful home by wretched intruders. They offer us treaties, but there is neither truth nor honesty in their pale hearts. The old chiefs were trusting and in an effort to show friendship and good-will, allowed them a path through our hunting grounds, a way for their 'iron road' to the mountains. We were told by their chief soldier, Gen. Harney, representative of the Great Father in Washington, that they wanted only a way to reach the western sea. But we allowed this dangerous snake into our midst. 'Surely, there is enough land for all,' I reasoned. In 1868, I was the last to sign the treaty, refusing until all forts were vacated in our territory. They promised that the Black Hills and the Little Big Horn would forever be Indian territory, set apart for our perpetual use. Scarcely was the ink dried on the treaty, when gold was found in the Black Hills. Even though they promised no white man could enter our land, we heard the sound of the white soldier's ax upon Little Piney. His presence here is an insult to the spirits of our ancestors. Are we then to give up their sacred graves to be plowed for corn? Dakotas, I am for war! Whenever we have trusted them, they have deceived us. Now we cry for vengeance. We will meet them with equal cunning. Show them no mercy. Whet your knives and string your bows! Sharpen your tomahawks. Hold your lances high. Paint your firm limbs and bodies -- streak your face with red berry clay. Let them tremble in fear as we approach -- the earth will shake as we rumble toward our enemy and the feathers of our war bonnets will flutter in the wind. Let the wretches die -- those who have stolen our land. We MUST BE FREE to roam over the soil that was our forefathers. Our songs shall rise among the hills, and every tipi shall be hung with the scalps of our foes. Those who have robbed and cheated us deserve our hatred and destruction. The White Man has made many promises, but has kept only one. He said 'We will take your land' and he took it. The land belongs to ALL people. It cannot be owned or 'allotted' as they desire."

These words of Red Cloud, following upon those of Crazy Horse and the other chiefs, roused others in the Council to demand vengeance. Whooping and yelling war cries, they brandished their weapons, jumping around in a circle, whirling like dervishes, their feet stamping in rhythm. Hideous yelps and battle cries, prolonged on a high shrill note, emerged from curled lips; while violently their hands and arms slashed through the skulls and torsos of imaginary opponents. The frenzy and fiendish sounds continued long into the night, accompanied by the howling of coyotes. If any whites were within hearing range, this wild scene would confirm what they already believed -- that these savages were a sub-human species, barbarians, an inferior being closer to the animals. They would be a fearsome and intimidating mass. When war-ready, they would emerge from the trees, splendidly mounted and painted for battle, in their fine array, waving rifles, held high, as well as lances and shields sparkling in the sun's fiery reflection.

CHAPTER 12

Emma Reynolds rose early at dawn to begin her chores which would continue throughout day until dusk which was her favorite time. That was because once all was completed, she could visit her children up on the hill. Donning her apron, she picked up the whisk broom in the corner by the rear door from which she could see lupines waving to and fro in the warm breeze out back, as well as delicate white, lily of-the-valley bobbing their tiny bell-shaped caps. Later she would gather some for her early evening visit. About to begin her work, she imagined she heard a cry -- like that of an infant -- but thought herself mistaken. The yearning for her lost children was so over-powering that she could still see them sometimes -- or at least imagine them -- before her eyes. But then she heard another whimper, come from the front porch.

Emma Reynolds found the infant in the cradle just as Black Elk had intended. In her bosom her heart leapt. Staring in disbelief, she wondered if her senses were intact. Perhaps this was an hallucination. Some months back she believed she had reached the break-ing point, insane with grief after the stillbirth. But now her ears and eyes were NOT deceiving her. Lifting this unknown miracle to her bosom, she removed her shawl from her shoulders, wrapping it around the baby, whom she placed upon her shoulder, against her thumping heart. Gently she patted the baby's back in circles with her free hand, while weeping in hope and joy and amazement. Could this be a gift from God to whom she had been praying for peace and acceptance? What other explanation? For a brief moment, in her shock, she imagined that she might be awakening from a bad dream; but this was a very-much-alive and squirming infant in her arms, kicking lustily and searching for a breast to suckle. Far off in the distant field she could see the bent figure of her husband Charles working the soil. He was a good man -- upright, honest, hard-work-ing -- although some considered him stern and humorless. But she knew him intimately; although a very private and serious man, he felt things keenly although he seemed unable to share his feelings. Upon the death of each child, he buried his grief deeper and deeper in frenzied, unrelenting work. From the house, she could see him ferociously chopping wood or mending a fence -- either hatchet or hammer wielded as savagely as a weapon; again and again and again it rose and fell in a crescendo of agony and bitterness. Following each loss, she had tried to reach out to him, but he did not respond. It seemed somehow he blamed himself for the brief and tragic lives of his children, as if he could have prevented the diphtheria or the pneumonia that claimed them. He had not touched her since the still-birth of the last -- he who had been so eager and passionate in the early years of their marriage. Despite his habitual silence, she knew his greatest fear -- to lose another child; surely his grief and guilt would break him totally this time. So now she hesitated to call his attention to this babe in her arms. How would he react? Did Charles have the strength to nurture another child only to anticipate a heart-breaking loss again? She could not fathom him any longer or predict his reaction. All she knew was that this infant needed nourishment, and so she set about to provide that. As she prepared to feed it, she tried to calm herself and began humming a sweet melody which made her smile for the first time in two years. Her mind was made up once she'd fed and changed the infant. While rocking him to sleep -- his soft down against her chin -- she knew she could never give him up, whatever her husband's feelings might be. She had found him and he was HERS for the keeping. Eventually he would be named Charley after her husband -- and Charley Reynolds would become the best and favorite scout for US Army General George Armstrong Custer.

CHAPTER 13

In early 1876, Gen. Custer was informed that Sitting Bull's braves were on a mission to collect a cache of both new and old weapons, including numerous rapid-fire Winchester, Henry, and Spencer rifles, as well as older muzzle-loading Leman guns. In addition, they had their usual tools of warfare: bows and arrows, Stone Age war clubs, and lances. They were able to obtain the guns through post-traders and gunrunners who worked out of the Dakota Territory. Even with just bows and arrows, which were effective up to 30 yards, US cavalrymen could be readily maimed or disabled. Imminent conflict was predicted, sooner rather than later. Also in the room was Gen. Alfred Terry who offered that his column out of Fort Abraham Lincoln contribute two Rodman and two Gatling guns for the expected confrontation with the Indians. Major James Brisbin concurred with Terry -- that it would be advisable to procure the formidable Gatling guns, since this awesome rapid-fire artillery was capable of firing 350 rounds per minute. But Custer did not like Brisbin and deemed the four-horse drawn Gatlin gun battery too cumbersome to drag over the obstacles of this terrain and estimated that valuable time would be lost assembling and disassembling them. Custer also cited previous problems with their use. On a reconnaissance mission in June conducted by Gen. Reno, they "had been nothing but trouble," and had actually been abandoned by soldiers who became fatigued dragging them over rough spots. In addition, they were known to jam due to a black powder residue that collected after several firings. Moreover, Gatlings, mounted high on carriages, required the battery crew to stand upright when firing them, easily exposing them to enemy sharpshooters. Custer declined the offer of these weapons and declared that if it came to war, he "planned to live and travel like Indians"; furthermore he was certain that his "7th Cavalry Regiment could handle anything" it met.

Custer's reputation was well known by the Indians, and they despised him. Known as "the boy-general with the golden hair," he had become a renowned leader in the Civil War back East and was considered quite a phenomenon. Despite graduating last in his class at West Point, he was adept in siege techniques, a supreme leader demonstrating good judgment, a brilliant tactician, gallant and ultra-courageous in battle. They had heard of the outlandish uniform Custer had fashioned for himself which screamed for attention: a broad-brimmed hat tilted to one side over his mass of long, wavy blond hair; a double-breasted velveteen jacket with gold piping, eight buttons on each side, embellished with five parallel lines of gold embroidery looped about the sleeves from forearm to elbow; and a bright red scarf flowing around his neck. He chose to stand out even in battle amidst clashing sabers, firing pistols, revolver blasts, stumbling horses, and colliding infantrymen. Both his soldiers and his enemy could spot him easily brandishing his sword, always at the front leading. Among the Indians, he had attained mythic proportions. They heard that he was protected by the spirits: one bullet bounced off his shoulder, merely bruising him. Although shots kicked up dust all around him, they always struck someone else to whose aid he would charge and bring back to safety. On one of these rescue missions, he was hit, but the round only grazed his head, stunning him briefly. Horses were shot beneath him and still he managed to survive.

Many of these feats had been mentioned at the council meeting between Chiefs Sitting Bull and Crazy Horse, where Black Elk was in attendance. Black Elk did not relish confrontation with the White Men as did some of the hostile young warriors. Finally, after a number of years devoted to White Dove's recovery, he had made her his bride and she had willingly accepted him. He had always displayed tenderness and patience with her, and she trusted him like no other. For their marriage he had presented her gifts made with his own hands: high boot-like moccasins, quilled with intricate designs and lined inside with rabbit fur for comfort and warmth; for protection from the cold, a hood made from caribou which he had deftly hunted and then designed to surround the delicate face he adored. For both of them, he fashioned a pair of earrings from porcupine quills and beads of semi-precious stones. They were light-weight, not heavy, for he did not want them to make her an *orejones* -- one with big ears stretched long by heavy ornaments. During the marriage ceremony he wore one and she the other as a symbol of their union -- hopefully forever. For storage of her special treasured possessions, he steamed cedar planks, then bent them and stitched them into place with cord to make a box. Elaborately he carved a cover, inlaid with shells of abalone. Such attention to a wife was not at all common among those in his tribe, so he presented his gifts to her in private. He also wanted to fully absorb alone the look upon her face when he bestowed them. Guiding her into the forest the evening before their marriage, he led her to a hollow tree. Repeatedly, he coaxed her to stretch her arm into this tree. She did not know for what she was searching; but seeing his lips curling in a mischievous smile, she reached deeper and deeper; and with each probing, she found another bundle. The very first contained an exquisite belt with much intricate beadwork in colors of cobalt, red, white and sunflower yellow, which spelled "I love you" -- a message he had "talked into the beads." Delightedly, like a child, she wrapped it around her narrow waist, touched by his unique expression of tenderness. His gifts displayed the keen aesthetic sense of an artist, for the color of the beads had been very carefully chosen and coordinated in a most compatible manner. This was not the ordinary, unimaginative courtship practiced by other men who would simply meet the girls of their choice at evening in front of the tipi. Enfolding the woman in his robe, their heads covered from view, they would converse, and perhaps kiss and embrace under cover, while children romped nearby and families came back and forth.

This was not the first example of Black Elk's unique creativity at sending her silent messages of significance. Some time ago he had led her on a sort of "hide-and-seek" game, requiring laborious climbing over the steep bluffs which ended in a granite cave. Leading her inside, he lit a torch which highlighted pictographs he had brightly painted on the walls expressing his feelings for her. She realized then her good fortune in being saved and chosen by such a one as he, for this was no ordinary man. Most of his tribesmen treated their wives as nuisances to be tolerated or adversaries to be conquered and quieted; at least that was what they seemed to demonstrate in their overt behavior. By a "beating-the-drum" announcement, some easily divorced those they considered lazy wives.

Now, to enable his beloved to find the other hidden "treasures," Black Elk lifted her in his muscular arms high up onto the limb of another tree. To gather these additional surprises, she had to climb higher to reach a hole bored into the trunk. And so it went -- a lovers' game of "seek and find." It was his lips that at the end she found -- the very best gift he had to give her, and she treasured his love and returned it with her own. How could she not respond to this most unique and unusual man who lived for her -- had waited only for her -- waited and waited and waited until she was ready to accept and return his passion. Within the year, they welcomed a new son whom they named Little Elk. For the adoption of this child into the tribe, his father fashioned for him a tiny earring made from gold found in the Black Hills, and so at the religious ceremony his ear was pierced to receive it. In addition, Black Elk had made a sort-of-amulet in the shape of a turtle from the baby's umbilical cord. He told White Dove it would give the infant a good, long life because the turtle represents longevity; for days after a turtle is killed, its heart keeps on beating and beating. At the ceremony, Black Elk's father who was the shaman, intoned: "Pray always to your parents for advice. No matter if you are calling from the depths of the earth, your voice will be heard and your appeal will be answered." At last, Black Elk had arrived at a good place in his life and was ultimately content, particularly with White Dove who appeared to thrive, suffused with ardor for him. In fact, he was quite certain that he heard a hint of a voice the first time he brought her to a climax. It thrilled him to not only pleasure her but with that, to activate her sound as well. It was only during their love-making that she reached the peak of abandon to allow herself vocal expression. At all other times, she remained silent; but he loved her unconditionally, satisfied that she had returned sufficiently to the land of the living. Although she had been making steady progress, it was the birth of Little Elk that had been the best medicine. As a new mother, she blossomed. Her face took on a glow that he had never seen before. Perhaps she had it as a child, but the brutal assault had erased all vitality; at last, she was coming into "the light."

CHAPTER 14

June 25, 1876

On June 25, 1876, Gen. George Armstrong Custer made his move -- he intended to attack in broad daylight at 12 noon although he had been warned of the size of the village. Leading a wing of his battalion, their sabers left behind as ordered, they wended their way down the Medicine Tail Coulee and towards the Little Bighorn River. Each soldier carried two standard weapons -- a Springfield carbine and a .45-caliber Colt revolver, but no bayonets or hand-to-hand weapons. Custer's intention was to ford the river, but the enemy was gathered closely on the other side. Custer's forces were divided into three battalions of differing sizes, his own the largest. Opposite the Cheyenne circle at the crossing, the division led by Capt. George Yates's approached the Indian families -- wives and children -- gathered at the north end of the huge native encampment of 1,200 lodges, plus several hundred wikiups of individual warriors. East of the village, hundreds of warriors surrounded a wing led by Capt. Myles Keogh, at the same time Capt. Yates and his men attempted to seize the Indian women and children. From his position on the ridge, Custer could see native warriors surge forward just as Yates' soldiers were almost within "striking distance" of the families. The Indian warriors spurred their horses forward to repulse them. Men led by Major Marcus Reno fired into the village, killing several women and children, while Indian warriors attacked the exposed left end of Reno's line. After twenty minutes of long-range firing, Trooper Billy Jackson came speedily to report that the Indians had begun massing in an open area, shielded by a small hill to the right of the village. Before he could finish speaking, 500 warriors attacked, sending Reno's men scrambling into the timber along the river's bend. Within minutes of the soldiers' retreat, the Indians set fire to the brush. Terrified soldiers, confused by Reno's orders to mount -- then dismount -- then remount again -- fled in disorganized bewilderment across the river by the steep bluffs. Many simply turned their horses loose while Indian women ran up from the village waving blankets frantically to scare away the cavalry horses. In panic, some soldiers threw down their weapons while Cheyenne and Sioux warriors rode them down.

A number of squaws finished off the wounded with eight to ten - pound stone mallets with rawhide handles. Custer's men, trapped and exposed upon the ridge on higher ground, were easy targets for the bows and arrows aimed in an arc over obstacles and the fog created by the puffs of smoke from the guns. All was mayhem. In the confusion Reno's Arikira Scout Bloody Knife, astride his horse next to Reno, was shot in the head, his blood and brains splattering the side of Reno's face. At the river's edge, twenty-nine troopers and three officers were smitten down as they tried to cross. Completely shaken, those who had retreated to the bluffs were fortunately met by Captain Frederick Benteen and his company arriving from the south, summoned by a messenger from Custer. Anticipating complete annihilation, they were relieved to see reinforcements approaching from McDougall's Company B. 14 officers and 340 troopers began to feverishly dig rifle pits in which to defend themselves. Some had fought earlier in the Civil War when anything available -- knives, eating utensils, mess plates, pans -- were utilized to dig. Benteen had a crucial decision to make: reinforce Reno's badly wounded and hard-pressed detachment or proceed toward the ridge to Custer, which were his orders. Benteen chose to go to Reno's aid even though Custer's messenger, Italian bugler John Martin (Giovanni Martini) carried him the handwritten message "Benteen. Come on, Big Village, Be Quick, Bring packs. P.S. Bring Packs." Heavy gunfire from the north indicated that Custer was engaged with the enemy in combat on the hill. Capt. Thomas Weir took it upon himself to go to Custer's aid and advanced a mile to the ridge, which would later be named after Weir. From the bluffs could be seen warriors on horseback shooting at objects on the ground. There were hundreds of them -- led by Crazy Horse, White Bull, Chief Gall, and others. Maintaining his calm, Benteen attempted to push back the Indians who were crawling through the grass closer and closer to the position of his soldiers. Courageously exposing himself, he was hit with a bullet in the heel of his boot. While these officers and their men were pinned down, Custer and his 210 men fought hard against the Lakota and Cheyenne. Some attempted to shield themselves behind breastworks made of their dead horses. Although Custer and his faithful men put up their most dogged defense, they realized all too swiftly they were doomed. Forty of his most loyal veterans made a desperate stand around their leader, delivering volley-fire at close range, but the Lakota swiftly killed all. In total the battle lasted less than one half-hour. One surviving Indian calculated the duration as about the amount of time "it takes a hungry man to eat a meal." The cavalrymen were simply overwhelmed -- outnumbered three to one. At the end Custer lay dead -- shot in the chest and the temple, surrounded by the bodies of his slain men, some shot, some with arrows protruding from their bodies, others with their skulls bashed in from the natives' stone clubs.

CHAPTER 15

Black Elk lay gravely injured on the battlefield. Two warriors carried him back to the village where he lay badly wounded in his tipi. He had seen Great Mother struck down in the first onslaught led by Capt. Reno against the women and children, during which he had swooped up White Dove and the baby, placing them out of harm's way.

Wildly, ferociously, he fought, striking left and right, plunging his lance into flesh and sinew, cutting down those who dared attack him. Puffs of gunpowder created a cloud of smoke through which it was difficult to see or breathe; but as he turned to face another foe approaching him, a bullet struck his left shoulder. Looking to determine its origin, he saw the scout Charley Reynolds focusing his gun a second time on Black Elk. He recognized the young man, for he had been secretly keeping a close watch on the boy since he had left White Dove's first-born so many years ago in the cradle on the Reynolds' front porch. Still Black Elk had the use of his right arm in which he had a stone war club. Turning his horse toward

Charley, Black Elk dug his knees into his steed, aiming for a full frontal assault. Charlie raised his rifle for a second shot, as Black Elk charged, his weapon held high in the air. Charlie struggled with the rifle, allowing the Indian time to reach him and to bash his skull in. But at the very last second, the Indian hesitated as if momentarily, paralyzed -- unable to actually make the lethal strike. Rather than swooping down in a cleaving blow upon Charley's head, with a blood-curdling shriek, Black Elk hurled the heavy club up high -- into the sky, far over and beyond the young man. Charley was momentarily stunned, aware that the Indian could have easily felled him, especially since Charley had become partly unseated in his saddle as he was pushed and shoved by the violent combatants who struck, slashed, struggled, and slipped in the carnage surrounding them. But that single moment of hesitation allowed the boy to right himself and take aim directly at Black Elk's chest, which he finally did. The bullet found its mark. The two were so close -- within arm's reach of each other; and with a strange look -- as if in recognition and ironic incredulity -- the Indian seemed to smile sardonically as his outstretched hand grazed the boy's shoulder, sliding down the length of Charley's arm to rest upon his hand. With this touch, skin upon skin, Black Elk fell from his horse to the ground. On his lips was the Sioux prayer: "Oh, Great Spirit, be merciful to me, that my people may live."

CHAPTER 16

Black Elk was glad that he had held White Dove close, nestled together much of the night before battle in order to tell her his wishes -- instructions of the utmost importance. It felt like the early months of their relationship when he had merely held her close all through the night. He seemed to have a premonition and there were necessary things to be said. Gradually, she had begun to speak again -- haltingly, uncertain, sometimes stumbling, stuttering over words -- but she had regained her voice after many years. He told her he did not want to fight, but fight he must. Their lives and way of life were threatened, and he must do his part. If he were to die in battle, he did not want her to grieve, for he was grateful for these years they'd had together -- both before and after their marriage. It had taken much time and patience to win her trust and heal her wounded psyche. And he had finally taken her as his bride by her own volition; she had come to him willingly at last. There had been many months after their marriage when he had simply held her close -- spoon-like -- in soft slumber. After a while lying behind her, he would stroke her back, her shoulders, each night before sleep enveloped them -- linked like this together, his large hand cupping her small firm breast. Exercising much restraint, eventually he had reached to touch her sensitive spot. Finding her moist, he ever so gently began rhythmically circling that spot, slowly, slowly, slowly -- then quickening, quickening with a bit more pressure. He could feel the beat of her heart against his chest as she pushed her body toward him, and still he did not take her. The ecstasy was mutual, nevertheless -- hers from the mounting pleasure he excited in her body -- his from the first sound he'd ever heard her make -- a whispered gasp when finally, she climaxed. And then -- later, frolicking beneath the thundering waterfall, he'd hoisted her up, her legs wrapped snugly around his middle. Playfully they submerged embraced together, then came up, submerged again. With water rippling round them, he'd slipped inside her ever so slowly -- for the very first time -- sliding inside, then ebbing out -- sliding and ebbing -- her hips undulating to match his movements. Placing her against the rock wall, he sucked upon her breasts as water cascaded down and between them -- first one nipple only, then the other. The heat of fiery passion, combined with the soothing coolness of the water, created a contrast of ecstasy. It was then and there, he believed she had conceived. He cherished their son born from this moment, her greatest gift to him, equal only to the gift of herself. And recalling together their first consummated love-making, she was to seek out that spot by the waterfall, for it was there that she would find his spirit. She was not to follow the mourning tradition of cutting off her hair -- that glorious, golden hair he so adored. It had been the very feature that so fascinated him when first he found her, for he had never witnessed anything like it before. The second, of course, were her eyes; when finally, they beheld him, he was smitten forever. She was to do NOTHING to deface herself as custom dictated. Let the other widows blacken their faces, torture their bodies by slashing their legs with cuts, and walk in procession, wailing and howling with their husband's jawbone attached to their clothing. He had always been allowed to walk his own walk; and as his wife, so she would too. She was the essence of beauty and she was to remain so. She was to keep herself healthy so that Little Elk did not become one of the *wablenicha* (orphan band). Nor was she to follow the tradition of "wandering to mourn" alone in the Black Hills to find the husband's spirit. He had told her where he could be found, at the waterfall, as part of *oy`ate* (the universe) created by *Wakan Tanka*, the Creator. There she should think about life and living, as it was there that life had begun for all three of their little family. Knowing that having died in battle, an Indian warrior was assured that he would soon be joined with the Great Spirit and borne into the infinite universe, she should be joyful for him. When she felt the wind upon her cheek, it would carry his kiss. When it blew through her hair, it would be his hand lightly ruffling it. Under no condition was she to enter those vile camps of relocation at the forts. They were ridden with filth, disease, and polluted water. Little Elk would not fare well there. Black Elk had observed these sorry, haunted places to which they took Indian prisoners who soon began to waste away from starvation and despair. Their people could not be "Blanket-Indians" -- those who steadfastly refused to adapt, nor could they demean themselves as the "Cut-Hair" who were inclined to willingly accept the rations of the government. So this was why there remained one more most significant task he assigned to her. She was to relearn her native language, for there would be more war, even if the Indians were victorious this time. It was written in the earth. The settlers, the ranchers, the homesteaders, the prospectors, the adventurers, the profiteers -- all would keep coming, raping the land until the Indian was driven out.

"There is change carried in the winds," he predicted. "They will offer treaty after treaty, and all will be unfair."

Her responsibility would be to negotiate wisely for their people -- for the future of their son. She must be the interpreter -- the representative -- her duty to carry the messages of what compromises the Indians could accept, but also allow them to retain their culture in order to remain true to themselves. She must speak for all of them.

He continued: "You know us best -- have lived for years among us and know our hearts. When the white men in government hear your story -- one of their own race who has loved us and been loved by us in return -- they will listen. Only you can make them recognize that the Lakota is not the brutal, uncivilized savage they are bent on annihilating. Instead we are a proud, fair, generous, family-oriented people who want only to be left alone to live our own way on our own land. Tell them that -- show them that. You are the living proof that both races can live together peacefully in mutual trust. Only you, in your unique position, can make them 'see,' and so you must. This will be your sacred mission, and I will be guiding your feet and your tongue." He kissed her deeply, adoringly, tasting the salt tears upon her cheek.

CHAPTER 17

As Black Elk had predicted, this was not the end of hostilities between the Indians and their enemy. After one treaty, when the provisions promised by the government arrived late and were substandard -- wormy, mealy flour and rancid meat -- a Sioux warrior Little Crow, enraged by the indignities heaped upon his tribe, went to ask the Indian agent Myrick where were the rations for the hungry Sioux. The agent's response: 'Let them eat grass for all I care.' In hurt pride and anger, Little Crow called for war against the Whites. In retaliation he led an attack on a German family gathered around a rough-hewn table piled with venison. Unshod pony hoofs drummed on the hard-packed earth outside. Painted Sioux crashed through the farmhouse door. Knives flashed, rifles fired. The farmer, his wife and child were hacked to death -- brutally, savagely -- the unchewed food still in their mouths. Then the Indians turned their attention to the agent Myrick who owned a store. With howling cries, the war party descended on it, slaughtering Myrick in his business and stuffing his mouth with grass, which is how he was found.

As instructed, White Dove did go to Washington, D. C. with Red Cloud, an impressive presence -- stately and regal bearing, dignified in manner. He had been dealt a lethal blow in 1865 -- hit in the back with an arrow whose head protruded from his chest. The injury would have doomed most men, but a Medicine Man had cut off the head and feather, and Red Cloud had miraculously recovered.

In the customary musical and agreeable voice, for which he was well-known, the revered Red Cloud spoke, translated by White Dove, on behalf of her "chosen" people, seeking justice for them; but progress and the desire to develop the West could not be stopped. In fact, Congress increased the size of the Army; and on August 15, 1876 passed the Indian Appropriation Act, which the Sioux called "the sell or starve" rider. All rations for the Sioux would be discontinued until they ended their defiance and ceded their beloved homeland -- the Black Hills to the United States. On his trips to Washington, Red Cloud became convinced that the number and power of the European Americans were so great that the Oglala had no choice but to make peace. Defeated, Red Cloud decided to devote his energy to helping his people transition from the freedom of the prairies to the confinement of the reservation. Unfortunately, they would soon become a broken people, defeated by a nation intent on "civilizing" them and separating them from their cultural heritage. In 1880, *yuw 'ipi*, their ancestral religious practices were declared illegal, and anyone practicing them was threatened with the "iron house" (imprisonment). In 1889 Congress annexed The Black Hills, the sacred land of the Sioux which once provided them with beaver, herds of deer, and bear whose fat roasted meat once provided food for many. The bearskins also provided warm clothing for the frigid winters on the Plains.

It was declared in that august chamber, the Senate: "The Indian can no longer stand as the breakwater against the constant tide of civilization ... An idle and thriftless race of savages cannot be permitted to stand guard at the treasure vaults of the nation which hold our gold and silver ... the prospector and the miner may enter, and, by enriching himself, enrich the nation and bless the world by the result of his toil." The earlier treaty that legally set aside the Black Hills as exclusive Indian domain, was that easily broken. Thousands of fortune seekers poured in, while 20,000 Indians living now on reservations, like Pine Ridge, some of the poorest land in the US, existed without jobs or industry. Here the "real" Native Americans, a once proud and independent people, were overcome with a sense of isolation, which diminished and, eventually, destroyed their sense of dignity and pride. Having lost their spiritual connection to the land -- their culture crushed and devastated -- many huddled in rags -- became despondent and hopeless, succumbing to alcoholism.

Desperate for some semblance of their former glory, some became adherents of a new form of mysticism -- the Ghost Dance religion which the government deemed subversive. The last and final confrontation occurred on December 29, 1890 at Wounded Knee, on the Pine Ridge Indian Reservation in southwest South Dakota where a group of Sioux warriors (about 106) were camped out and were part of a group being moved to a reservation in Omaha. They were ordered by the US Army to relinquish their guns. In addition, the soldiers intended to arrest their chief Big Foot. As the soldiers searched through the warriors' belongings, a gun accidentally went off, triggering shooting on both sides. It ended with the death of unarmed Sioux families -- mothers, children -- who happened to be at the camp. Soldiers with guns followed them as they ran along the clay bank, and fired their guns repeatedly. They did not consider whether their guns were aimed at armed warriors or unarmed families. By the end, women and children lay heaped and scattered along the gulch and piled into a mass grave. "A people's dream died there." In total 300 of the Sioux were killed, in addition to 25 soldiers.

In the 1950s Pres. Eisenhower declared "termination" -- attempting to force the Indians off the reservations and into major cities; but these Indians found only poverty, minimum wage employment (if any), and urban "Red" ghettos. At least on the reservations, a man could hunt, kill a deer, fish to help support his family. In a city he was out of his natural element.

In the early '60s, Pres. John F. Kennedy considered naming one of the "41 for Freedom" ballistic missile submarines after Red Cloud to honor his leadership and diplomacy; but the Pentagon was concerned that the name could be misinterpreted as being pro-Communist.

In the mid-'70s the basketball star Bill Bradley attended a basketball clinic at the aforementioned Pine Ridge Reservation and became aware of their tragic history. Later when he was elected to the US Senate, he introduced legislation that would return 1.3 million acres of the land taken from the Indians by Pres. Grant. Bradley had met with Charlotte A. Black Elk, an Oglala Sioux and member of the Black Hills Steering Committee, comprised of eight tribes of the original Sioux nation. At that time Bradley also spoke with 96-year-old Emma Plenty Wolf Hollow Horn and learned that this stolen land -- 7.3 million acres, taken in a treaty ratified in 1868 -- is known to the Sioux as *"wamakas og'naka i'cante,* the heart of every-thing" (interpreted by Charlotte Black Elk). As part of that agreement mentioned previously, Congress created the Great Sioux Reservation, almost half of South Dakota. (A portion of that land is now Mt. Rushmore, where the visages of four Presidents are carved into the granite.) In 1980, The Supreme Court admitted that the US had wrongfully seized the Black Hills from the Sioux; and in an attempt at restitution, offered a payment of one-hundred million dollars for that territory, but the Indians refused to accept the settlement. What appears to have been totally ignored is that fundamental to the Indians is their spiritual connection to that land. They said they will "never abandon their claim" to the Black Hills; it is "not a matter of dollars and cents." Gerald Clifford, Charlotte Black Elk's husband, said "The Lakota see the earth as their mother. It provides both spiritual and material needs." Today this sacred spot has become the site of the largest motorcycle rally in the United States.

Acknowledgements

This is a short novel of historical fiction. Although set against the actual background of Westward expansion and its resulting problems with the Native American population, this story of Black Elk and White Dove is entirely a creation of my imagination, although there was an Oglala Sioux warrior by the name of Black Elk. In addition, there actually was a white child captured in 1864 and raised among the Indians; later she married a respected warrior with whom she chose to remain. I did make use of real characters who were involved with the historical events. For example, there were indeed actual Chiefs Sitting Bull of the Sioux tribe and Crazy Horse, as well as Red Cloud, White Bull, and Gall. Red Cloud, who eventually became the spokesman for the remaining Indians, did go to Washington, D. C. to plead for his tribe; but, of course, there was no White Dove with him since she was a creation of my imagination. Gen. George Armstrong Custer did lead his US Army 7th Cavalry Regiment to fight the combined Indian forces at the Battle of the Little Big Horn and was warned early in 1876 by his favorite Scout "Lonesome" Charley Reynolds that Sitting Bull's forces had been amassing weapons, including Winchester repeating rifles and ammunition. Reynolds was actually born in1842 in Illinois, but was not the son of Black Elk and White Dove, as depicted in my story; nor was he adopted and raised by a couple, Emma and Charles Reynolds. Nor was there a homesteading family headed by Alex and Sarah Jenks, although there were many families who went westward seeking opportunity and a better life for themselves. Also true is that all in the 7th Cavalry, including Custer and Reynolds, were annihilated at the Battle of the Little Bighorn. It was said that Reynolds "fought with valor and fidelity -- before falling gloriously, fighting for his country." As for the dispute regarding whether or not the Gatling guns would have affected the outcome of the battle, although some military experts at the inquiry following the battle said these weapons had drawbacks, such as jamming, others testified that they "functioned surprisingly well." Like scout "Lonesome" Charley Reynolds and the Indian chiefs mentioned above, the following WERE also REAL people who lived and participated in the events described: Gen. Alfred Terry; Captains Myles Keogh and George Yates (both killed in battle); Captains Frederick Benteen and Thomas Weir; Majors James Brisbin and Marcus Reno; Mary Brave Bird; Reno's scout Bloody Knife; Trooper Billy Jackson, as well as Emma Plenty Wolf Hollow Horn; Gerald Clifford and his wife, Charlotte Black Elk, whose later testimony was given to basketball star, Bill Bradley, later a US Senator and who did exert effort to right the wrongs inflicted upon the Sioux. Charlotte Black Elk was not, however, the daughter of Black Elk and White Dove. Interestingly enough, I had chosen Black Elk for the name of my gallant and noble Lakota hero long before I read that there was actually a real person by the name of Charlotte Black Elk. I suppose I could have contin-ued the story using her as the granddaughter of my fictitious characters, White Dove and Black Elk, but I did not. In addition, there was a real female Crow scout named White Dove who was severely wounded in The Battle of the Little Big Horn; however, I chose that name for my main female character before I even knew of this real woman. The

Battle of the Little Big Horn, as well as that of Wounded Knee, are regrettable events in our national history and ones the Native Americans have deeply etched in their memories.

Following the earlier battle, 120 men and women appeared claiming to be the lone survivor of "Custer's Last Stand," but none was ever given credibility by scholars and historians. It was believed that all of Custer's men perished. An investigation was launched following the battle, and it was never determined whether or not Custer intended to ford the river. According to Pretty Shield, wife of Goes-Ahead, a Crow scout for the 7th Cavalry, Custer was killed while crossing the river and died there in the water. In her account, Custer was slain by a Lakota named Big-nose. But according to testimony by Chief Gall, Custer never attempted to ford the river; the closest he came to it was his final position up on the ridge where his body was supposedly found. This version was supported by other Indians, including the wife of Spotted Horn Bull. It was concluded that this was true since there were no bodies or horses found near the ford. According to the Cheyennes, the blow that knocked Custer from his horse was delivered by Buffalo Calf Road Woman. These contradicting accounts have fed speculation for years as to Custer's chosen route and will probably never be resolved. To the best of my ability, I have tried to relate historical events as they most likely happened and did extensive research to insure this, using Wikipedia, in addition to such texts as *American Epic: Story of the American Indian* by Marriott and Rachlin; *Ohitika Woman* by Mary Brave Bird with Richard Erdoes; *Dictionary of the American Indian* by John Stoutenburgh, Jr.; *Native Americans and the Reservation* by Anita Louise McCormick; *The Woman Who Lived With the Wolves* by Paul Gobel; *Custer's Trials: A Life on the Frontier of New America* by T. J. Stiles; *Kennedy* by Theodore Sorenson; and a 1987 article in *The New York Times* about Sen. Bill Bradley's visits to the reservation at Pine Ridge. Any errors in the relation of the events are entirely my own although I made every effort to insure their accuracy.

DONATELLA ANNUNZIATA CONCETTA D'ALESSANDRO

DONATELLA ANNUNZIATA CONCETTA D'ALESSANDRO

An Odyssey from Federal Hill (Providence, RI) to the Amalfi Coast

PART I

Donatella Annunziata Concetta D'Alessandro was a big girl with a big name that she did not like at all. In fact, today as she made her way home from school, there was not too much that Donatella liked about herself or her surroundings; for Donatella lived in a rather crowded section of Providence, Rhode Island -- the Italian section known as "Federal Hill." It was certainly colorful enough -- all kinds of food and cheese shops, meat markets, "pasticcerias," "trattorias," and "ristorantes." Usually Donatella enjoyed the attractive displays, the hustle and bustle, the sights, sounds, and smells of her neighborhood; but today she ignored all she passed. Up at the top of the "HILL," was her parents' market; and even from this distance, she could see the large piece of white butcher paper taped to the store front window advertising in large black magic marker "Provolone - $4.59 /lb, as well as "Mortadella," "Prosciutto," and "Salami." Sometimes, "Ella," as she was called for brevity, would stop here before proceeding the next two blocks to her home. But through the window she could see her Mama and "Babbo" (Daddy) busy waiting on customers, and right now 'Ella did not really want to encounter the observations and remarks of these same patrons. Through the glass she could see Mrs. Prezioso, a robust, red-faced matron, shouting out her order, item by item, as Babbo worked feverishly slicing mounds of cold cuts. At the counter her mother was bagging ravioli, manicotti, gnocchi, escarole, and cannellini beans, also on Mrs. Prezioso's list. Every week it was the same list, and it seemed that Mrs. Prezioso's life was as boring and routine as her list. 'Ella dreamed of exotic, faraway places she read about in books: Paris, Rome, London -- anywhere would certainly be more interesting than here. Sneaking around the corner, she made her way unnoticed across DePasquale Square, actually a sort of piazza with a unique sculpted stone fountain. A cool mist sprayed her cheek as she passed close to its cascading water. This WAS one place 'Ella loved from her earliest days when her "Nonno" (grandfather) took her there for walks on summer evenings after "la cena" (dinner). Young couples strolled arm-in-arm, some sat sipping cappuccinos under brightly striped -- red, white, and green -- umbrella tables. Mothers proudly pushed carriages containing plump, ruddy-faced infants cradled in exquisite hand-crocheted, pastel-colored shawls that spilled over the sides of the pram. Old ladies, dressed all in black, sat on benches in the square, gossiping in the dialect of their native "paesi" and reminiscing about the "old country." But best of all was the music. On certain nights a trio -- accordionist, violinist, and soloist -- would position themselves in front of the fountain and perform classic Italian arias -- melodious tunes -- "Torna a Sorrento," "O Sole Mio," "Santa Lucia," which would not only be appreciatively applauded, but also bring a misty- eyed look to her Nonno and other immigrants. They would hum along or nod their heads in unison to the rhythm of the tune, as she and Nonno stood hand-in-hand enjoying it all. He would often tease her that perhaps tonight the "gelateria" would not have the particular flavor she was craving -- gelato all'arancia -- since the visit to the ice cream shop was the highlight of the evening. But today as she passed the place, it held no appeal for her. Arriving home, she headed to the back yard where she knew she would find Nonno tending his garden. 'Ella loved this peaceful haven from the busy world outside -- and she found comfort in its neat and ordered rows of cucumbers, zucchini, lettuce, tomatoes, peppers (red, green, and yellow) -- a kalei-doscope of vibrant color. Nonno spotted her from behind the tall corn he was spraying. As she approached, he took in her solemn, tear-stained face.

"Carina," (Dear one), "vieni qui." (Come here). Reaching out he took her hand and led her to the little wooden bench beneath the grape arbor in the corner of the garden. Heavy clusters of vines draped around the white lattice arch, creat-ing their own private hideaway. Reaching upward, he plucked a handful of juicy red-purple grapes, extending them to her in his weathered bronze hands. She shook her head, refusing his offering. Dropping the fruit into a straw basket on the bench, he drew her closer.

"Come va?" (How are things?) "Perche dolorosa?" (Why so sad?)

"Oh, Nonno, do you remember the story you used to tell me about "Pumadora"? (Little Feather). Tell it to me again now."

And her grandfather who was intuitive and observant, began, "Once upon a time, many decades ago, there was a little girl who was s-o-o-o very thin -- just skin and bones -- because she did not like to eat. Her mama would cook for her the most delicious foods ('Delizioso') and decorate them to entice her daughter's appetite, but to no use. As a result, Pumadora grew thinner and thinner and thinner, lighter and lighter and lighter, until she weighed no more than a feather (*pumadora*). So that is what everyone began to call her, 'Little Feather.' One cold day when she ventured out of her house to play, suddenly a strong gust of wind swept her up into the air and through the sky carried her for some distance dropping her on the porch of a tiny house -- just big enough for her -- in the middle of a deep forest. When Pumadora had caught her breath, her curiosity got the better of her, and she tried the front door which was unlocked. Once inside, she realized that the house and everything in it was made of salt and pepper cubes -- sort of like small black and white bricks. After her long trip, she was very, very thirsty, found a glass and went to the sink. Filling her glass from the faucet, she tilted it to her lips and drank. UGH! It was salty water! Although unable to quench her thirst, she was extremely hungry -- very, very unusual for her. Searching around the kitchen, she found a loaf of very dark, hard bread and took a chunk. To her great disappointment, it consisted entirely of hard pepper, which caused a body-wracking coughing jag.

"Oh, Dio mio!" she wailed in hunger, fatigue, and frustration, and she began *piangere.*

"Oh, mi scusi, Donatella. 'Piangere' means to cry.'"

"I know what it means, Nonno," Donatella interrupted impatiently. "Go on with the story."

"It had been a very long day indeed. She also missed her mother and father, yearning for their comforting hugs. Eyeing a small bed in the corner, she lay gingerly upon it and -- 'Lo and behold!' -- it too was a rectangular hard slab of salt. In great discomfit, she sobbed herself to sleep; but first she prayed that if God would help her get home, she would eat all her meals and fatten up so this would never happen again. Awakening, she WAS at home in her own bed with her mother embracing her. "Pumadora," she said, "you must have been having a very bad dream."

"Oh, yes," confessed the child. "It was the very worst nightmare in the entire world! Now I am very hungry for breakfast. I'd like some eggs, bacon, toast, fruit and cereal..." She stopped at her mother's look of amazement, since this was a most unusual request for Pumadora.

"You want ALL THAT? I will make it if you think you can finish it."

"OH, YES!" asserted Pumadoro, "and also from now on, I don't want anyone to call me by my nickname, 'Pumadora' anymore."

"E` finito," (Finished) said Nonno. "Basta!" (Enough) and clapped his hands.

But Donatella was not smiling. Instead she emitted a long sigh and confided, "I wish I could become like Pumadora."

"What! Why would you want that?" Nonno exclaimed.

"Because, Nonno, all the kids at school tease me and laugh at me. No one likes me."

"What don't they like? You are a fine girl -- truly wonderful -- bellissima (beautiful)."

"No, Grampa," you are wrong." She had switched to her American name for him which she used only when she was very serious. "I am definitely NOT beautiful. Today Giorgio and his friends made up a song, especially about me."

"See," retorted Nonno. "How nice of them."

"N-o-o-o-, Grampa," she wailed. "You DON'T see!" and she began to chant:

"Donatella non e bella (Donatella is not pretty.)

Il babbo venda mortadella. [Her father sells mortadella (ham).]

La mamma somiglia una patata (Her mother resembles a potato.)

Donatell'e` grossa ragazza." (Donatella is a fat girl.)

"Oh, *Poverina*," (Poor girl), consoled Nonno. "They are young fools. They do not know what beauty is," he declared with a reassuring hug.

The following day -- Saturday -- Nonno led her down Federal Hill in the direction opposite from their usual nightly strolls. The bottom of Federal Hill was no less colorful than the upper part -- the sidewalks lined with fruit vendors whose carts were overflowing with juicy red strawberries, tart blackberries, sun-drenched oranges, prickly pears, crimson pomegranates, just ripened cantaloupes, all varieties of apples -- artistically displayed in pyramid stacks.

"Boun' giorno," greeted the proprietor, Signore DiMezza. "Uno momento."

He was assisting Signora Tucci weigh her fruit selections on a gargantuan metal scale hanging from a chain.

"Non e` necessario," replied Nonno. "We can help ourselves." This was one of Nonno's habits -- switching between Italian and English in the same sentence.

When his granddaughter asked why he persisted in this, he explained, "Ah, Carina, I forget. My tongue starts speaking Italian before my head reminds me I am in America," (pronounced "Ah - mer- ee - car -" rolling the r).

First Nonno chose a melon after shaking many of them.

What are you doing?" asked Donatella.

"Well," he replied. "I am giving you a lesson. You pick up the melon that is the least green -- mostly coral color -- and shake it next to your ear. If it is ripe and sweet, you should hear the liquid swooshing inside."

Proceeding down the hill, he asked Donatella for three of the oranges from their basket and started nimbly juggling them. "How do you do that while walking?" marveled Donatella, amazed at his agility.

"Oh, I learned it as a boy in the old country. In the town square in front of "Il Duomo" (the Cathedral) I would perform. Sometimes I juggled four, then five. People would gather and applaud and drop coins in the hat I had placed on the ground in front of me.

"Why did you do that?"

"Because I was poor -- very, very poor, and I was on my own."

"What do you mean -- on your own?"

"Alone in the world," answered Nonno. "It was after the war."

They had reached the bottom of "The Hill" where it led into the city of Providence below. Across from "Providence Place" shopping mall was a small oval ice skating rink and park surrounded by a small stadium. The Providence River had recently been re-routed, and little bridges resembling those in Venice had been built to connect the various parts of the city. It was a lovely spring day so they found themselves a bench under blossoming pink Japanese cherry trees. A shiny ebony gondola floated down the winding river. Another one with a black patent-leather sheen was at the dock where passengers waited to take a ride.

"But how did you survive?" asked Donatella.

"Basta." (Enough of the past) "I like it here," declared Nonno. "It reminds me of Venezia."

" Were you born in Venezia?" persisted Donatella.

"No," replied Nonno. "I was born in Conca dei Marini, in Italia on the Amalfi Coast."

As Nonno began to hum a familiar Italian melody, he pared an orange in a circular motion. She did not realize until he placed it around her ears, that he had cut the rind in such a design that it fit perfectly as would a pair of glasses. Then he did the same for himself, and placing them around his ears and perched on his nose, he leaned closer to her face, growling a line from "Little Red Riding Hood" where the wolf says, "The better to see you with, my dear" just before he jumps up to eat her. Donatella threw up her hands, feigning horror. She giggled delightedly; she never tired of Grampa's cleverness nor his games and stories. He was lots of fun and she enjoyed her time with him. Finishing the sweet oranges, they made their way home climbing back up the hill. Nonno patted his granddaughter's cheek lovingly and whispered, " Ti amo."

PART II

The years passed. One day, Mamma was unable to stand up for long in the market waiting on customers. In just a few months she was gone. Less than two years later, when Donatella was in her senior year of high school, Babbo also died. Now it was just she and Nonno. Actually it had always seemed to be "just she and Nonno" since her parents had given all their time and energy into making the market a success -- it was their livelihood -- it sustained all four of them, although Nonno contributed all the produce for the store from his large garden.

One day soon after her father's passing, Nonno suggested they take their nightly stroll after 'Ella had completed her homework.

"Carissima," began Nonno, "you are an exceptional student and you should have a promising future."

"Ah, Nonno," sighed 'Ella. "I can't see any future ahead. Everything feels dark -- black -- no color in my world. I just try to get through each day. I feel like a zombie. I didn't even cry at Papa's funeral."

"Poverina," Nonno put his muscular arm around her. "You are still in shock. What you feel is normal. You have lost those dearest in your life."

"That is what I struggle with, Nonno. YOU are the dearest one in my life! If I were to lose you, I would be lost. YOU have been with me every day as far back as I can remember. Mama and Pappa were so busy at the store; and when they did come home at night, they were so tired -- worn out -- Mama slowly dragging her feet up the stairs and Papa stooped and weary."

"Si, (yes). I know," sighed Nonno. "That store was their dream. They took it on together; and when you came along and Mamma saw you needed care, they sent for me. The year before, I'd lost your "Nonna" (grandmother), and I was swallowed up in grief. Your nonna was my life; you are named after her you know -- a fine woman in every way. I knew your mama needed me; she said it was my chance to "taste" life again. And so I came -- left everything -- actually what I cherished most had been ripped from me and I felt not even half alive. And then, when I first saw you -- the almond shaped eyes, the long silky eyelashes -- even your complexion was hers -- I was entranced -- your smile -- hers too -- was enchanting -- and my heart filled with something -- love, I guess -- life renewed. You were a gift. I even ventured to guess -- maybe even sent by her. God works in strange ways, you see. And so you are the dearest thing in all the world to me."

Wrapping her arms around him, the tears -- so delayed -- finally began to fall. He held her in his broad embrace and let her cry -- a good long, cleansing cry.

The following day, he broached the matter he had been pondering for some time. Since she and he could not manage the store, and since there were interested buyers, would she consider selling it along with the house; after all it was her inheritance.

"But where would we live, Nonno?"

"Well, my child. You must have a future. You have a keen mind which should be exercised. You MUST go to university."

"But where? How?" she queried, afraid to get her hopes up.

"Well, this next you must consider carefully, for it is your future life, not mine. I still have my cottage in Italia -- Conca dei

Marini -- a pretty little place -- charming -- as your grandmother made it for me -- it is filled with her essence. We could live there this summer after your graduation in June, and then -- with the money from the sale of the store and house, you can attend university -- perhaps Bologna or wherever you like. But you would be leaving your home here and everything familiar to you."

"Oh, Nonno!" she protested adamantly. "YOU ARE MY HOME! I do not need time to decide. It would be a great adventure -- a future -- a beginning. Mille grazie!" (A thousand thanks).

"Oh, no, Carina. It is for **YOU** that **I** owe thanks."

PART III

"**M**adonna Mia!" exclaimed 'Ella delightedly some months later, as they approached Conca dei Marini, the "pretty little place" between Positano and Amalfi where Nonno's house was located.

"You never told me about ALL THIS BEAUTY! How did you ever leave it?"

"For you, Carina. For you."

They had climbed the rolling hills above the port town, quite a trek; but magnificent views of the brilliant blue iridescent water below, touched by the sparkling sun, created a kaleidoscope of glittering fragments on the surface. As they approached from the sea, the first blush of sunset cast its warm glow on the golden and terracotta facades of the houses. Navigating narrow interlacing alleyways, 'Ella caught glimpses of lush tropical-like palm foliage peeking out behind black iron-gated courtyards. 'Ella was glad she had worn rubber-soled shoes for the ascent up the cobbled paths required stepping gingerly. Somehow Nonno seemed rejuvenated. Eagerly, energized, he led -- far ahead of her because she was trying to absorb the gorgeous landscape which left her breathless -- to the point where she was speechless. Her emotions in a whirlwind, she was overwhelmed with the spectrum of color spread out before her. The jagged granite cliffs seen from the boat were magnificent enough, as well as the coastline sprinkled with enchanting hidden beaches laid out before cave-like openings in the rock. It mesmerized her -- the dreamy stretch of rugged coastline and now verdant outcroppings everywhere. As they ascended, the stepped maze of narrow byways gave way to wider spaces. Nonno paused to allow her to catch up and turned toward the sea.

"La bella vista! Magnifico!" and so it was -- a sweeping panorama of sea and sky.

Giddy with sensory over-load, 'Ella could only utter, "Bellissimo," inadequate as it was for such a glorious paradise. Church bells began to peal, tolling the hour.

Nonno said, "It must be 6 o'clock -- the Angelus." Then he bowed his head, lost in deep reflection, allowing 'Ella a few moments to look down at the chiseled landscape as if from a towering precipice, creating a physical sensation that she was actually floating over the sea. She too should pray in gratitude, she realized; but this was all too much for her. When Nonno moved again, she just followed mutely, as if in splendored shock. Wildflowers carpeted the gently rising hills, and a cool evening breeze carried with it the faint citrus scent of lemon trees.

Then suddenly Nonno turned right and focused far ahead upon a two-storied white-washed dwelling, surrounded by bushes of fragrant lavender and jasmine. A pair of tall pointed cypress stood sentinel on each side of a brightly-painted cobalt blue door. Arched above the door was etched "Casa di Gioia" (House of Joy). Tears formed in Nonno's eyes. Massive patches of ivy clung to the stucco sides, overlapping thickly entwined vines. To Donatella's eyes it was a house from a fairytale -- the whole thing a magical scene. As Nonno led his granddaughter toward the back, emerged more lavender bushes sprinkled throughout a vegetable patch; agapanthus covered an artistically designed and well-manicured garden -- a gem of horticulture.

"La mia bella sposa." (My beautiful, beloved wife). Nonno sighed deeply and wiped his brow. Beyond the garden were rows of silvery olive trees from whose scent Nonno savored a deep lungful,

as if breathing from an oxygen tank necessary to sustain life. Donatella already sensed a change in him -- all the way up he had climbed
quickly, rejuvenated, as if on a quest -- unaware of leaving her many
steps behind. Of course, she had been trying to take it all in -- so
new to her, so familiar to him.

Entering the cottage beneath a stone archway, Donatella in-
stantly saw a carefully nurtured home. Lovingly hand-made and
cleverly designed items had been artistically placed in just the right
spots. Above the stone mantle and also in the kitchen were exquis-
itely colorful Majolica. Some mosaic painted tiles had been included
in the backsplash of the kitchen counter top. One in particular -- the
bright face of some deity, set in a sunflower-sun, winked back at her
from a dazzling navy-blue glazed background. Cobalt and yellow
pottery brightened the kitchen table; one lovely pitcher was filled
with sunflowers from the garden and sat upon a pristine lace
trimmed linen cloth with corners of hand-stitched floral bouquets.
Nonno lovingly caressed the corners.

"Who tends to all this?" questioned Donatella, since everything was fresh and cared-for.

"The dearest friend of your grandmother has readied this for
our arrival. She is very excited to meet you. She and your grandmother were very close since childhood; and she has seen that all
was maintained throughout my time with you in America.

"Let me show you your room." Nonno led her through another archway to the well-worn stairs. Along the walls were hung
lovely small oil paintings -- one scene was the front of the house
with large red-scarlet geranium pots on each side of the cobalt-blue
front door, a vibrant contrast of color. Another was of the back terrace -- looking down on their property rolling down below to the
olive grove, the tips of the silvery leaves delicately highlighted in a
pale yellow-white, as if kissed gently by the sun. At the top of the
staircase was one with the view from the bedroom, although Donatella did not realize this until she entered the chamber. From the
glass-paned French doors, she took in the splendor of the landscape.
Moving through them to the second story balcony, she saw in the
distance an ancient barn. A cool breeze brought the smell of hay,

intermingled with the scent of juicy fig, lemon, and orange trees surrounding the periphery of the garden below. From her high perch, her eyes lingered over the turquoise sea beyond, traversed by yachts, motor boats, and varicolored fishermen's craft, which, from this height, appeared like dots upon the horizon. Parting her lips, she gasped, "Oh, Nonno! You never told me about this!"

"Carina, this house is the work of your grandmother. She laid out the gardens and everything else. When she acquired it, it was in disrepair -- nearly in ruins. It is a long story. SHE named it 'Casa di Gioa' and it was indeed that while she was here. But when she passed, I could no longer see beauty or color. Everything was dark -- a blackness overtook me. I could not rise from bed. I was alive, but not living. Amelia, her friend, came every day with broth and fruit and whatever else she thought would woo me from my despair, but to no avail. I didn't bathe or shave or eat. What I hungered for had been wrested from me. I had no purpose; everything I had ever done, I did for her. SHE was my purpose -- my energy. She had saved me once from oblivion and only she could save me then. Hopeless, lethargic, I wasted away in grief and nothingness. 'Niente.' Until that letter came -- the letter from your parents. Amelia brought that too because I no longer collected any mail. I had cut myself off from the world. And she read it to me as I still lay morose upon the bed. 'This is your chance,' Amelia chided. 'SHE has surely sent you this babe named after her. As SHE once saved you from yourself long ago, SHE has again come to you through this child. Go, Vincenzo! Rouse yourself. You are needed. Corraggio! I will send word that you will go.' And so she did, and I meekly followed her arrangements. I had no energy myself."

"Ah, Nonno, I had no idea. You always seemed -- if not happy -- at least content."

"You, Grandchild, you changed my life. And as you grew, it was uncanny how much you resembled her. And so I did believe -- SHE sent you to me when I most needed a reminder that my time was not yet done."

"No, No," she insisted. "Mama and Papa had little time for me. I do not blame them. You gave me all your time -- always."

"I didn't know your parents were struggling so. Your Dad, my son, was bored here, feeling confined in such an isolated place -- bound in by cliffs and sea. He received letters from a cousin in America boasting that the "streets are paved in gold" and there were opportunities for young men like him. Your grandmother was broken-hearted when he left -- our only child -- but he had just married your mother who too was eager for adventure. And so they left. We were consoled that at least they had each other; for we believed, as in our own case, that two people in love, together can make their dreams come true."

Turning from the outdoor terrace, they re-entered the bedroom. On an iron bed lay a hand-crocheted coverlet, its center a pattern of entwined hearts.

"She made that too -- your grandmother, an eternal romantic. She HAD to be if she married ME!"

"Why do you say that, Nonno?"

"Because my beginnings were not fortuitous -- I think that is the English word to say ' I was not considered a good catch.'"

"Oh, Nonno, I can't believe that. Not at all."

"Believe me, child. But SHE believed in me and gave me faith in myself. I could never disappoint her. And she gave me all the care I never had. She was over-flowing with tenderness and love -- an endless fountain. But let me show you the rest."

Every nook and cranny in the house had been impeccably considered. There was attention in the details. Colorful, intricate tapestries covered some walls -- the designs a masterpiece of artistry. Hand-hooked rugs of guled colors lay scattered on the unpolished floor boards. A dainty white organdy skirt hung in soft folds from the boudoir porcelain sink. On a shelf was a silver-rimmed photo of Nonna and Nonno in their younger days. "My God!" 'Ella felt she was looking at her own image. The similarities were striking. Why had Nonno never shown her a photo like this? All her life, her grandmother had seemed like some remote, ethereal being apart from this world, and yet she had created all this "living" space -- imbued with her very essence which surrounded and permeated all.

Later in the evening, sitting on a rough-hewn bench beneath the grape arbor, Nonno announced that they would have a visitor. It was a tranquil evening, and soon arrived a tall and elegant lady, very unlike some of the more robust females they had encountered on their trek uphill. She had her silver-streaked hair tied back casually in a chignon and a gorgeous light-weight fuchsia shawl draped around her shoulders. She had a very patrician bearing and in her long and graceful fingers she took Donatella's.

"My Dear," she spoke English with just a trace of an accent. "How I have waited in anticipation to finally meet you. I am Amelia." She gazed at Donatella with such fondness as if they were already intimately acquainted. Feasting her eyes, slowly, gradually, Amelia took in all of Donatella, nodding appreciatively. Fondly, she touched Donatella's shoulder, her hand warm and gentle.

"Ah, yes!" Amelia sighed nostalgically, clearly moved, and glanced with tears at Nonno who seemed to understand all within that sigh.

"Let us go into the garden and sit. I will bring some drinks," suggested Nonno.

Amelia strolled first in and out of the garden's sections, circling one and then the other. Purple bougainvillea languorously draped the wall where she took a seat on a wrought-iron loveseat.

"Your grandmother designed this Eden," she began. "She was a masterful gardener, among her many other talents. When we were girls, I tended to be jealous of her. She was so good at everything she undertook, but it was impossible to harbor any ill will -- envy or otherwise -- toward her. She was too sweet, too kind, too wise, too good -- the 'real thing' as you say in America. She treaded with an air of authenticity, and she exuded an infectious love of life which others derived from her -- particularly your grandfather. I genuinely feared he would not live long without her. He might not have, if not for your arrival. He was an orphan from the war, impoverished, raised by nuns. He often ran away -- many times -- was lost -- without direction -- "un monello" (street urchin) -- living on the streets -- without a family or a future. Your grandmother defied her parents to marry him. And with her, he was – 'come si dice?' (how do you say it?) -- he was re-born. She was truly the love of his life. I was so shocked to see how closely you resemble her -- like a young version resurrected. I hope that does not make you uncomfortable."

"No, but Nonno has told me none of this. He never mentioned her until we came here."

"Ah, Donatella, there are reasons. He was bereft when he lost her -- could not cope with her absence from his life. She was EVERYTHING to him; and I believe that in order to survive, he had to keep her to himself. The pain of sharing his memories and past would have shattered his composure. I was entrusted to maintain everything as she had created it, and so you still see her touch on all."

Suddenly Nonno emerged from the house bearing limoncello in hand-painted glasses that Amelia seemed to recognize. Later, 'Ella learned they had been a wedding gift from Amelia.

PART IV

Summer passed idyllically. Donatella was accepted at La Universita` di Bologna to study design, and Nonno encouraged her to go. He would be here awaiting her return -- here in Conca dei Marini (Seafarers' Basin) on holidays and vacations. Actually he told her that some called it "Conca di Ciello" (Heaven's Basin) for its incredible peace and beauty. Moreover, it had always been considered ideal for "buen retiro" (good retirement) because it was sublime spot for bucolic comforts. It may also have been why her restless father yearned for a more exciting life. During these past months, Nonno had acquainted her with much of the history. It was a favored location of skilled sailors and fishermen who found their livelihood in its bountiful emerald waters. The special coral was in great demand and divers came just for that. In addition, Nonno presented her with her grandmother's cook books, replete with original recipes, many of which 'Ella tried. Nonno complimented her profusely and seemed to grow more robust with each of her gastronomic creations. They often ate "al fresco" on the terrace with its glorious view of the sea; and the table was always meticulously appointed with her grandmother's colorful dishes, glassware, and cutlery. Vibrant multi-colored bouquets of flowers, fresh from the garden, adorned the table; and herbs -- thyme, parsley, and rosemary -- were liberally sprinkled onto the dishes. 'Ella learned to use anchovies and capers. The diet was varied, according to her grandmother's notes that instructed "variety is the spice of life." One day 'Ella, like her Nonna, might serve "stoccafisso" (salted cod); another night "vegetariano," basically (vegetarian); and always a plate of home-made pasta -- spaghetti, macaroni, intorce, pappardelle -- in a savory sauce made from the juiciest tomatoes prolific just steps from the back door. Soups were hearty and tasty, always garnished with *pecorino* or *parmesan* cheese grated over the plate just before serving. One soup was made of layers of black bread, butter and *fontina* cheese, stepped first in broth and then baked in the sturdy brick oven. Nonno really favored this soft *fontina* cheese and liked it as an appetizer with hard-crust bread, dipped in extra virgin olive oil made on their own presses. Chicken was reserved for Sunday or sometimes there'd be a pig with a crown of spicy sausages. She even ventured to marinate a hare (rabbit) in rosemary and Barolo wine which Nonno hadn't had in years. His wide grin spoke volumes. Though his broadest smile was reserved for a favorite dish -- a single large snail on his appetizer plate -- and he knew she had gone down to the wharf to obtain it. Her "tiramisu" and "torta del Paradiso" were scrumptious. Assiduously following her grandmother's recipes, she mixed butter and eggs, flour, sugar, and flavored it with lemon rind. 'Ella did her best to reciprocate his years of devotion to her -- to nurture him in every way; and so he was reminded of his time with his own Donatella and he was happy -- very happy. The young 'Ella was also completely content -- perhaps for the first time in her life. She seemed to blossom in this setting, as if she had found her "real" home. She felt her DNA was in THIS place, and now it was inscribed upon her senses. And she became acquainted with her grandmother. In the margins of the recipe books in a neat script, Donatella would find telling notes: "Eat deliciously, but wisely", "Good taste and good balance of foods should be the rule for healthy bodies"; "Truffles are one of the undisputed pleasures of life." Her Nonna lauded the virtues of rice: "easy to digest; a cure-all for stomach ailments," as well as its "medicinal effects for those suffering from high blood pressure." And her best advice of all: "Serve with a sweet smile" and remember "To an Italian, carefully prepared food is an offering of love." A similar sentiment -- "Love wisely and love well" -- was also embroidered on the pillow sham in the bedroom. It had been "their" room -- her grandparents, but Nonno had bequeathed it to her willingly. He said he could not sleep in it without "la mia moglie" (my wife). And Donnatella came to know her grandmother, whose name she now bore proudly; and not only treasured her recipes, but also her loving advice, as if her grandmother had somehow sensed she would take her place here. But what silly meanderings! How could her grandmother have possibly predicted this and left these little notes for her?

In September, she descended to the town center below -- "Citta dei Navigati." It was not her first time. She had often wandered the cobbled streets, getting lost in the myriad alleyways, discovering little treasures that always delighted her. She and Nonno had sometimes dined at the enchanting beachfront cafes in nearby Ravello or Amalfi, surrounded by the ambient murmuring of conversations. She had embraced the local traditions, even participating in the religious festival in August, had traveled to toney Capri, and environs. But now it was time to begin the next chapter of her life.

Little could she have imagined how changed her life would be when she arrived for study at Universita` a Bologna. At first she was overwhelmed by the large and busy city after living in a serene seaside village. It seems she had just adapted to her new location in Marina dei Conca when she was dropped in La Piazza Maggiore, Bologna's nerve center where City Hall, the palazzo of Podesta, and the Gothic cathedral of St. Petronius all faced onto it. But it was here that she met Claudio, also in Bologna for the first time and also a student at the Universita` where he would study finance and marketing. She would bring him home to meet Nonno, eventually they would marry and start a thriving enterprise. She would pen cook books that would bring her an international reputation as a result of Claudio's brilliant advertising maneuvers. Together they would open a renowned cooking school, catering to up-and-coming chefs worldwide, as well as other gastronomic enthusiasts. Theirs would be a full and happy marriage, and Claudio would think her beautiful, confirming what Nonno had tried to impress upon her all those sad and lonely years before. Nonno had made her the confident woman she had become -- he had always supported her, given her a home and a future in a new location, and loved her unconditionally. Together with Nonna's recipes and cookbook "messages," Donatella had learned to "Love wisely and love well!" - which indeed she did. "Bravo!"

COPY-CATTING

COPY-CATTING

Louise slammed down the phone. She was furious. Virginia had DONE IT AGAIN! Louise reasoned that she should feel flattered, but she was NOT! She was irked. She and Ginny had been best friends throughout girlhood -- spending time together at each other's house, working together on school projects, going to the movies, to the beach, enjoying each other's company, helping each other. Why, if she hadn't had Ginny for her lab partner in chemistry, she would have never passed the experiments, nor the course. Louise always knew her friend not only liked her, but also admired her sense of style. She would often very overtly look Louise over from head to foot, especially when Louise wore a new outfit. Louise knew she had her own unique style, an innate sense of what went well together and what looked good on her. In addition, she had a flair. Somehow she knew a flowing scarf around the neck would look dramatic, or a piece of chunky jewelry make a statement. She had this unerring sense of fashion, so she knew when Ginny gave her that very obvious "once-over" -- often "twice and three times over" -- her friend was appraising her. It had really never bothered her; it felt nice to be admired and know that she looked good. But

Ginny never said a word to that effect or paid any compliment which was OK with Louise. She did not need affirmation from Ginny; and through college and after, they remained friends although not like the intimacy of younger days.

And then "IT" started! Louise and her husband were building their dream-house -- an authentic French country style with a four-sided Mansard roof, each side with two slopes. Louise liked old-world architecture; and in their town of ordinary colonial and split-level houses, it would look distinctive. After perusing house and garden magazines like *Veranda* and *Architectural Digest* for years, she was ready. Louise chose a plan and then went to town adapting it to her liking. The exterior would be a combination of pale gray stucco and limestone with pairs of long vertical windows flanking a heavy paneled oak front door. She favored symmetry. She delighted in searching for just the right antique pots in which to place charming topiary trees she'd seen in European landscapes. Next, she tackled the interior, leaving nothing to chance. For the living room she designed handsome mahogany bookcases flanking the fireplace and chose exquisite fluted molding to enhance them. For the handsome double-sided stone fireplace she provided the mason with a picture, and he duplicated it exactly. Oh, was she having fun! She had waited a long time for this. She combed shops for miles around searching for just the right objects d'art and accessories to enhance the look she was hoping to achieve. Her surroundings were very important to her; she gave as much time to her bedroom, which only she and her husband would see, as to the public rooms below. She so enjoyed exercising her creativity and imagination in myriad ways -- culinary, decorative, attire -- considering them all means of self-expression. Their project took a full year to complete, but it was indeed "a labor of love" -- so pleased were they with the results. It was THEIR FIRST HOME, and she took pride in the fact that it certainly reflected "her personal touch." Of course, as is customary in such cases, Ginny, as well as other close friends, came to visit, bearing house-warming gifts. Eagerly Louise showed them around, pointing out all her careful selections. She felt great satisfaction in the results of her effort and imagination.

AND THEN "IT" STARTED! Some time later, Ginny married and began to build her house -- a French mansard two streets away in the same neighborhood. When Virginia went to reciprocate with a house-warming gift ... Lo and Behold! In the dining room window was a mahogany tea-wagon just like Louise's with the drawer open from which draped leafy shiny green philodendron. It had been a clever, creative touch but IT WAS LOUISE'S TOUCH!

She began to distance herself to some degree from Ginny because Louise did not like the negative feelings she had begun to harbor for her "friend." Although she chastised herself for being "silly," somehow it still bothered her.

And then for a special anniversary, her husband surprised her with a gift she had been coveting -- a full-length cat-lynx coat. Such a luxury! A very special gift indeed! She was delighted, and he had insisted she don it with nothing beneath, and turn this way and that way under his ardent gaze, until she threw her arms around him in very happy gratitude, which led to another type of "gift-giving," actually "warmer" than the coat! It didn't get much use that winter since the weather had been mild, but she anticipated enjoying it much more the next year.

AND THEN! Who should appear at the holiday party in the very same coat, same style -- but Ginny! This really was the limit! Louise scolded herself for being "petty" -- but somehow that did not work to assuage her disappointment. She attempted to rationalize that Ginny was certainly entitled to a fur coat if she liked, but WHY that same fur coat??!! There was sable, fox, chinchilla, beaver, mink -- brown, black, autumn haze, gray, patterned -- so many different kinds of fur -- so many shades! Immediately the expression "two-for-the-price-of-one" popped into her head, and next "a dime a dozen."

Somehow the "specialness" of the coat was diminished. All the way home, Louise chided herself, "It's only "a thing" -- an "object" -- "nothing significant;" and yet her annoyance would not subside.

She thought the final straw was the DIAMOND! When they had married, Louise and her husband were young and poor. Both knew only that they were very much in love. Little else mattered except being together. So when their 25th anniversary date was approaching, her husband suggested that they go to the jeweler for what he would have loved to give her all those years ago if only he could have afforded it. Again she was delighted, as well as touched, since it was his suggestion and wish to please her. Together they selected an outstanding, high quality, large emerald-cut diamond set in platinum and flanked by three baguettes on each side -- a truly exquisite gift. Her husband joked that "that was IT" until their 50th and she was thrilled.

Some time later at an event, they encountered Ginny and her husband. They were all holding glasses of wine, and then Ginny's husband said, "Ginny, show them your new bauble." LO and BEHOLD -- an emerald-cut diamond, but set in yellow gold. Was this a coincidence? Louise was dismayed. She and her husband had together spent hours choosing something unique. He knew that she favored things that were "different" - not common or "run-of-the mill," and he had been so happy and willing to compliment her tastes.

"WHAT WAS THIS ALL ABOUT??!!" she wondered. This competition, if that's what it was. Louise was glad for Ginny's good fortune, really. She certainly was entitled to reap the rewards of a lifetime of hard work and a good marriage, as had Louise. But WHY always at Louise' "expense," so to speak? It just always spoiled the joy of it all. Louise felt defeated.

AND NOW THIS! The final straw. Cecile from the "boutique" had called to say the dress was ready. Louise had purchased the finest lime-green silk shantung fabric while on a trip and brought it to Cecile. She thought she'd like the dressmaker to design for her a two piece ensemble, with a flared skirt and wrap-around V-neck top with a contrasting sash at the waist. She'd brought with her the coordinating fabric for the sash -- a really "cool" interesting tiny plaid of yellow and turquoise. This very striking combination, as well as the diamond broach she planned to use to hold the sash in place, would be a "knockout," she was sure. As the seamstress carefully took her measurements, Louise could visualize the finished product. And soon the dress was ready. She rushed down to the shop. As she slipped it on, suddenly she was no longer sure the color suited her. Posing in the mirror, turning left and right -- left and right again -- she felt her intuition for once had failed her. Finally, she removed the lovely creation, telling Cecile she needed a bit more time to decide. Aware that it had been custom made for her, she was willing to forego the 50% deposit if she decided not to take it. Cecile complied since Louise was a very good patron and had never been uncertain before. In addition, Cecile had garnered a lot of business not only from Louise herself, but also from the many admirers of her customer's fashion sense.

So soon after, when she had called Cecile at the shop to say she would be in to reconsider the dress, she was incredulous to learn it had been purchased.

"By WHOM?"

"Why, Virginia," responded the seamstress.

Frustrated, irritated, bursting with resentment, she decided a confrontation was long overdue. Impulsively she phoned Virginia.

Without preamble, she stated: "I understand you purchased MY dress."

"Oh, yes," replied her friend, feigning innocence. "It is simply divine. I just adore it! It needed just a bit of alteration. I plan to wear it to the fundraiser at the club. Isn't your husband the chairman for the event? What will you wear now?"

Sardonically mimicking Ginny, she replied, "WHAT will I wear NOW? Why in the world would I ever tell YOU? So you can rush right out and SCOOP UP that one too??!!"

"Pardon me," responded Ginny. "Are you angry --- you sound angry? I thought you didn't want the dress?"

"WHY do you DO this?" accused Louise in desperation.

"Do what?" queried Ginny.

"COPY ME! The house, the fur coat, the diamond...." she trailed off exasperated with Ginny's denseness.

"Oh, my!" whispered Ginny. "I've really never given it much thought, but probably because I've always admired you so -- your innate sense of style. You look just great all the time. Your home could be a spread in a magazine. Whatever you put your touch on is a 'winner.' I'm never sure what looks good, so I guess I feel safe picking up tips from you. I know I can't go wrong then. I never re-alized it offended you. I am s -o-o genuinely sorry. I WON'T wear the dress. You may have it back," she bleated contritely.

"No, YOU wear the dress," replied Louise, a feeling of em-barrassment overcoming her. She did not like herself at the moment -- she sounded petty, "catty," materialistic. Virginia's adulation was sincere -- she'd seen it every time Virginia's eyes swept over her from head to toe. Louise had allowed this to affect what had been a true and deep friendship. This was superficial stuff. She felt ashamed. Their close relationship had waned, and she missed Vir-ginia; in fact, she missed her a lot.

She sensed her friend sniffling on the other end.

"No, Virginia. I should be apologizing to you. Forget this conversation. I do not like seeing you upset. See you Saturday night at the event."

And she DID indeed see Ginny at the gala --- in the striking lime silk dress. In fact, it looked better on Ginny than it had on her. It suited her friend well. Just FABULOUS -- a diamond broach pinned on the left side at the waist, holding the sash in place. Now WHERE did Ginny ever get that idea!!?? Louise nodded and smiled at her friend across the room.

Poetry

PREFACE

On the "Dedication" page at the beginning of this book, I identified the influential individuals who fostered my love of the written word, and many are the same who helped tune my ear to the cadence of poetry. I mentioned earlier my love of the Brownings -- both Elizabeth Barrett and her husband Robert, who fell in love with her poetry long before he even met her. She was an invalid, bed-ridden and confined entirely to her room by a tyrannical Victorian father who fully exercised his patriarchal control over his children, none more than this daughter Elizabeth. It was believed at the time that a fall from a horse had caused her injuries from which she seemed unable to recover. The only things that sustained her spirit were composing her own poetry and waiting eagerly for the publication of Browning's. He too found in her poetry a kindred spirit and wrote letters insisting on a meeting. She delayed and delayed to allow him an audience, until she could no longer deny his persistence. For the incurable romantic in me, I took such delight in their personal story since he rescued her from that dark, drab, and dreary home where she lived in complete isolation with only Flush, her little dog, for company. With Browning, she eloped to Italy where they wed and went on to enjoy many happy years together with a son conceived and born there. Perhaps that glorious period in his life enabled him to write so optimistically in *Pippa Passes*: "All's right with the world!" and for her to write to him: "How do I love thee? Let me count the ways..." My husband, well-knowing my inclinations, once many years ago sent me a Valentine card with that poem cataloguing all the things she adores about her spouse, and I have kept it to this day.

In contrast to this British couple are more modern American poets who equally appeal to me in quite a different manner. William Carlos Williams, a pediatrician who wrote extremely brief and succinct thoughts on his prescription pads, as well as e.e. cummings, whom my high school students liked because he eschewed capitalization, punctuation and traditional stanzas. Instead he scattered his words every which way down the page, coining new words and phrases: "mud-luscious"; "puddle-wonderful"; anyone lived in a pretty how town, with up so floating many bells down ... someone married their everyones"; "Buffalo Bill's defunct, who used to ride a watersmoothsilver stallion..."

While Williams was overtly simple, cummings was obscure, leaving the reader to puzzle over and interpret the lines for himself

I recently completed a book *The Road Not Taken* by David Orr who attempts to analyze the meaning of the poem by that title and the intent of the poet Robert Frost who composed it. Orr suggests that so many critics and analysts get it wrong. Some insist that the line "I took the road less traveled by, And that has made all the difference" indicates an independent spirit who defies convention. Another believes that, of course, it is about making a significant choice at a crossroad in life: "Two roads diverged in a wood, And I took the road less traveled by." However, rather than being a declaration of self-assertion, some believe it is the poet's attempt to convince himself that, looking back many years later, he initially made the right choice.

The Road Not Taken

Two roads diverged in a yellow wood,
And sorry I could not travel both
And be one traveler, long I stood
And looked down one as far as I could
To where it bent in the undergrowth;

Then took the other, as just as fair,
And having perhaps the better claim,
Because it was grassy and wanted wear;
Though as for that the passing there
Had worn them really about the same,

And both that morning equally lay
In leaves no step had trodden black.
Oh, I kept the first for another day!
Yet knowing how way leads on to way,
I doubted if I should ever come back.

I shall be telling this with a sigh
Somewhere ages and ages hence:
Two roads diverged in a wood, and I—
I took the one less traveled by,
And that has made all the difference.

~Robert Frost

Why do I mention these very different poets each with his own very unique style?

First, as an introduction to my own collection of poems that follow and to assure you that mine, unlike the puzzles that e. e. cummings and Robert Frost present, are quite straightforward and focus primarily on my own musings and experiences.

"Viva, Buon' Appetito" was inspired by my attendance at a wedding of a young couple and wondering what life had in store for them.

"City Scene" came to me while stopped at a red light at a busy Florida intersection where homeless people slouched on and beneath a bench waiting for the city bus.

"Regret" was triggered by a young woman who realized very soon after marriage that it had been a major mistake.

"Whose hands are these?" arose from a memory of my grand-mother.

"Sleep" is probably the most personal since I suffer from sleep apnea which keeps me awake many nights.

"Wife and Mother" is also very personal since those are the roles I have most valued and cherished in my life.

"The Poet's Lie" refers to one of Robert Browning's optimistic poems to Elizabeth in which he wrote "Grow old along with me, The best is yet to be." And for them it was true since the second half of their lives was so much more fulfilling than the first part. But for most people, the reality is that aging contradicts that expectation.

"Altruism" imitates the form of a poem by William Carlos Williams, a poet mentioned previously.

> "So much depends
> upon
> a red wheel
> barrow
> glazed with rain
> water
> beside the white
> chickens"
>
> ~ William Carlos Williams

When I would introduce Williams to my students, the common reaction was "I can do that!" And, of course, they could and did; I encouraged them to experiment. They often began with "So much depends on my allowance..., my parents..., air..., God..., my bike..., my car..., words..., money..., where you are born...

I encourage you too to contemplate this cue: "So much depends upon....." It will certainly get you thinking.

VIVA BUON' APPETITO!

Oh, to be young again!
  With everything yet ahead
So much to come
        But one can never guess the future
The bride and groom
        make promises in naïve hope and trust
May Life be good to them.

But Life's a pie of many portions
        and serves up a slice of joy some days
        children
           birthdays
              anniversaries
                  holidays
                      milestones

On others
    trouble
        adversity
          and disappointment

Be steadfast, strong
        As you taste each slice
            Both sweet and tart
The sweet will nourish
        And the sour make you stronger

But do not attempt
        to consume
          it all at once,
            as it is too much to digest

Nibble the apportioned single slices slowly
        savoring some
          swallowing others
            without grimacing

Until the pie is gone
        and you are satiated

ALTRUISM

So much
    depends upon
Altruism
    Without it
        man's baser instincts would prevail
Selfishness and greed
        would cloud one's eyes
            to the misery of the forlorn
who struggle and cower
    beneath
        poverty, subjugation, illness and ignorance

Without it
    would anyone respond to the pleas of the world's forsaken?

FIRST KISS

Pertly puckered lips

        tantalizingly pink

            quivering

                    inviting

Pursed and sensuous

        delectably teasing

              whispering

                  coaxing

                    ready to accept the kiss

Nipping gently in reciprocation

BETSY ROSS

Diligently you stitched by candle light,
Could you foresee the future symbolism of that unfurled banner?
Rippling in the wind for all to see
First, a beacon welcoming immigrants to unfamiliar shores
Later, above the sands of Iwo Jima, on Normandy Beaches,
Vietnam, Afghanistan and Iraq
Wherever democracy was threatened
Finally, shrouding the remains of courageous patriots
Who made the ultimate sacrifice.
Stalwart, it waves lustily, defiantly in the fickle wind
Declaring that "all men are equal,"
entitled to "liberty and justice for all"

OLD THINGS

The satin sheen
      of Great-grandmother's table
           Duncan-Phyfe mahogany
               With its gracefully carved fluted legs
Gives testament to
      generations before me
           who dutifully polished it with elbow-grease
              to enhance its lustrous finish
A valued heirloom
      treasured through the years
           by those who came before me
              but now unwanted
My children do not
      "see" its beauty
           nor appreciate its history
They prefer
    modern chrome and glass
           functional
             utilitarian
               sleek
                geometric
                  clean-lines
Stark representations
      of a "newer" age

They need
    Lord Byron's eye
        to realize
        "A thing of beauty
           is a joy forever."

OPTIMISTIC ROBERT BROWNING

Optimistic

Robert Browning,

You were lying

When you stated,

"Grow old along with me;

The best is yet to be."

For most, however,

The opposite is true --

The Italians have it right --

"Vecchiae e corona" (Old Age is ugly, brutal)

In ways too numerous to count

Stooped gait, arthritic fingers, dim eyesight, limited hearing

So much diminishment -- indignity

But still we push on and endure

Uncertain of the future

PLANTATION HOUSE

It stands aloof
        alone
           among the giant sycamores
Ancient oaks stand sentinel
              around the once grand edifice
A ghostly, sepulchral white
Its piazza circling the periphery
               where once little-uns spread their toys
                 and played their games upon the columned porch
At eventide
      crisp linen-suited men
              lounged languidly against the railing
                sipping ice-frosted mint juleps
                  cursing the oppressive remnant heat
Sweat-soaked
      yearning for cacophonous claps of thunder
               announcing respite rain
A neatly trimmed boxwood hedge
            once framed the cobbled walkway
               strewn with doe-soft pink magnolia petals
Jasmine
    gardenias
        honey-suckle
            all combined to make a heady fragrance
Now
   only phantasmagoric shadows
             slink furtively around
               cob-webbed ante-bellum chambers

REGRET

She lies awake in this unfamiliar bed,
        Baffled by everything she feels --
                or didn't feel.
Married just this morning
          to the sleeping stranger beside her;
There had been no incredible passion
            nor tender coupling.
There had been nothing at all.

She fears her restless rustling might rouse him --
             her husband. HER HUSBAND!
Reality pierces her brain --
          Jars her to consciousness.
How had she let this happen?
       "Hush, my quaking heart,
           lest he awaken!"
She'd so prefer a solitary chamber
       than this --
          imprisoned by his leaden arm across her chest.
Through the open window
       she spies a sprinkling of stars
           against the velvet sky.
The room is bathed in twilight.
       She squeezes tight her eyes
          to end the pulsing in her temples.
Oh, if she could be borne aloft
       into that celestial firmament outside!
Whatever's to be done now?

He moves -- then turns away from her.
       Stealthily she slides across the bed,
         staggering in the dark,
           against the portmanteau left open on the floor
From which she takes some clothing,
        dresses in the dark,
          and slips out silently.

SLEEP

Sleep

    precious, unattainable

Dream-rest

The balm to which "The Bard" referred

      that "wraps up the raveled sleeve of care"

eludes me once again.

Ambien, Sominex,

    ineffective -- all for naught

There is no "off" switch for my mind

Morning comes too soon

WHOSE HANDS ARE THESE?

Whose hands are these?
                     wrinkled, arthritic, and blue-veined
Trembling -- spilling everything they hold
                           fingers stiff and gnarled
               Useless for buttoning
How long have they been thus?
               Which once were smooth and creamy
                      fragrant with lavender scented lotion
"Oh! so very soft!" he used to say.
               But strong enough
                   To hoist a precious babe upon the hip
               And lift the weighty iron pot
                   From off the blackened grate
               To scrub on corrugated wash board
                   Come laundry day
               And vigorously sweep
                   The floorboards inside and the porch outside
               Grab oozing udders in the barn
                   To milk the bursting, swollen-bellied cows
               Then lug laboriously
                   Splashing, weighty pails across the frozen ground
These hands were never idle
               Knitting, mending, sewing -- come eventide
             cooking, cleaning, child-ing by day
Do they remember?
               That soon will be forever still.

CITY SCENE

Stopped at the light
        I see them
                waiting for the bus
Bearded
     Disheveled
             Dirt-encrusted wrinkled faces
                                Wasted visages
Counting out their change
                for food or beer?
With crutch one hobbles to the graffiti-covered bench
He needs much more
            than just one crutch
                     to support him
                          in his daily struggle to survive
I wonder what he may have been before
                   Secure?
                     Solid?
                       Upright?
                          Productive?
               OR
Doomed from childhood?
            To slog along in life
                  Unloved
                     Unknown
                        Uncared for
Abandoned by the unforgiving world
                precariously balanced
                    between life and obscurity
    Between poor
          and
            poorer
               dark
             and
               darker
Light turns green
        I catch them
                in my rearview mirror
Boarding the bus
        to nowhere

FEMALE AUTHORS

Jane Austen,
      Charlotte Bronte,
            Elizabeth Barrett,
                  Emily Dickinson,

How did you exist in such intolerably restricted times?

Did you not feel imprisoned both in mind and body?

Could that be why you sought the pen to liberate your thoughts and feelings?

Ah! Such freedom to abandon them to paper
                    Wistful
                        Wild
                            Romantic
                              Yearnings

5 AM

In the pre-dawn darkness
                    I sit in stupored silence
As I await
          the test results
The future is precariously balanced
                         between
                                   Benign / MALIGNANT
Life devolved
          from just two words
They sober and awaken me
                    preparation for
                              an unknown fate

PROGENY

Grandchild,

    I knew you before

        you were even born

Child
  of my heart
      my hope
        my dreams
          my imagination
            my DNA
              my future

Assuring my continuance

    and

    immortality

HOPE

So much
    depends upon
HOPE
    especially when you
                  hesitate
                        paralyzed by indecision or fear
                              of future consequences

HOPE urges you to
            FORGE ahead
                into the UNKNOWABLE future

MUSINGS

Infinity
    Eternity
        Omnipotence
            Incomprehensible concepts
                for finite human beings

  No beginning
      No end
The Soul
    The Spirit
        The Universe
           Of what substance are these made?
In puzzlement and awe
        we wonder,
           contemplate
These enigmas
      So beyond
         our limited knowledge
            and
              human comprehension

TRUE FAITH

True Faith
      is certainly a gift
               That soothes the troubled soul
              Calms the anxious
               Lifts the depressed
                 Carries the defeated
                  Lightens the burdened

If only one believes
          Steadfastly
             Unwavering
That he is not alone
         That Someone guides his steps
           And sees into his deepest soul
             Knows his overwhelming fears
             Understands his doubts

The crushing weight he endures
         Will be nevermore

And he will say
        "Unto, my Lord, I commend my spirit."

UNKIND WORDS

This is just to say
　　　　　your words have pierced my heart
　　　　　　　　and stung my senses
　　　so undeserving and unkind

But you are stolid
　　　　　in your stubbornness

So
　　　no apology
　　　　　　will be
　　　　　　　　forthcoming

WIFE AND MOTHER

Snuggling by the evening fire
        Making love upon the carpet
                she vacuumed earlier that day
Checking on the sleeping child
        kissing the tiny head
             with tousled hair
Later
  waking to a plaintive cry
         placing a hand upon his fevered brow
Come morning
      light frosted snow upon the icy, hardened ground
Bundling up
     for a visit to the pediatrician
           RX obtained and administered
12 noon
   bubbling soup upon the stove
          wafting comforting aromas
Baby's belly full of wholesome broth
       lethargic napping on the couch
She gazes adoringly
      upon the heavy-lidded eyes
         and crimson cheeks
When suddenly
    he stirs
      reaching upward
        to her
         as limbs upon a tree
Stretch out toward heaven
      to kiss the sun
Soothingly she cuddles him
     in a strong embrace
        Her angel
         upon whom
          she feasts her eyes

ENGLISH CLASS

I stand before my teenage students
  Speaking of Homer's "Odyssey"
Of Penelope, Ulysses' faithful and long-suffering wife
  Who waited twenty years for reunion with her husband.
Before me sit teens who fall in and out of love each week.

I laud "The Bard"
  Shakespeare and his masterpieces
The boys see only the curvaceous "masterpiece"
  Of the svelte but buxom female blonde
Who floats across the room.

I speak of poets
  Byron, Shelley, Keats
"A thing of beauty is a joy forever."
  They nod approvingly
As the same female student sauntering back to her desk
  Deftly demonstrates "poetry in motion"

"Remember John Donne
  who wrote "No man is an island unto himself."
And with that quote, they recall the hijinks
  Of last week's boozy island beach party
With bombed-out babes.

"Do I cast pearls before swine?" I wonder
  The bell rings – class ends
A student approaches and requests that I peruse his poems;
  I take them home; that night I read them.

Can it be that this sleepy-eyed tattooed boy
  Has actually "heard" me?
He writes "A thing of beauty"
  The Statue of Liberty that welcomed him from a distant land.
Ruled by some "MacBeth-like" tyrant – ruthless and ambitious.

And identified with "No man is an island"
   When a church group sheltered his family
And led him to this place
   Where in due time, he plans to "march to his own drummer."

And so my teacher's "heart leaps up
   when I behold" not Wordsworth's "rainbow in the sky"
But rather one single student
   With whom these works have resonated
Words that will be written
   On the masterpiece manuscript that will become his life.

www.ingramcontent.com/pod-product-compliance
Lightning Source LLC
Chambersburg PA
CBHW071128250626
47159CB00006B/2168